D0324313

Latin American Monographs

Second Series

Land Tenure and the Rural Exodus in Chile, Colombia, Costa Rica, and Peru

19

Center for Latin American Studies
University of Florida

To The Chief
And
The Bananas Over The Fence

Land Tenure and the Rural Exodus in Chile, Colombia, Costa Rica, and Peru

R. Paul Shaw

A University of Florida Book
The University Presses of Florida
Gainesville-1976

Latin American Monographs—Second Series

Committee on Publications

W. W. McPherson, *Chairman*
Graduate Research Professor
of Agricultural Economics

R. W. Bradbury
Professor of Economics

Raymond E. Crist
Graduate Research Professor
of Geography

Paul L. Doughty
Professor of Anthropology

Lyle N. McAlister
Professor of History

Felicity Trueblood
Assistant Professor
Latin American Studies
and History

Library of Congress Cataloging in Publication Data

Shaw, R. Paul.
    Land tenure and the rural exodus in Chile, Colombia,
Costa Rica, and Peru.

    (Latin American monographs; 2d ser., no. 19)
    "A University of Florida book."
    Bibliography: p.
    Includes index.
    1. Rural-urban migration—Latin America—Mathemati-
cal models—Case studies. 2. Land tenure—Latin Ameri-
ca—Case studies.   I. Title.   II. Series: Florida.
University, Gainesville. Center for Latin American
Studies. Latin American monographs; 2d ser., no. 19.
HB1990.5.S5   301.36'1   75-40048
ISBN 0-8130-0528-0

SPONSORED BY THE
CENTER FOR LATIN AMERICAN STUDIES

COPYRIGHT © 1976 BY THE BOARD OF REGENTS
OF THE STATE OF FLORIDA

All rights reserved

PRINTED BY THE ROSE PRINTING COMPANY, INCORPORATED
TALLAHASSEE, FLORIDA

HB
1990.5
.S5

Acknowledgments

JULIAN WOLPERT (Princeton University), John Durand (University of Pennsylvania), and Richard Easterlin (University of Pennsylvania) have provided invaluable advice on a variety of methodological problems to do with the logic of economic and demographic interrelations. I am particularly grateful to Julian Wolpert for his encouragement throughout all stages of this study. To Ernest Landauer (Berkeley, California), I offer special thanks as he has been instrumental in my interest in the developmental problems of Latin America.

The financial support of the Ford Foundation and the Population Studies Center of the University of Pennsylvania has enabled me to complete this study uninterrupted. Sylvia Sacks of the Inter-American Statistical Institute (Washington, D.C.) has been extremely helpful in granting me easy and efficient access to a great deal of Latin American census and survey data. Louise Kantrow (New York) has also helped me in many ways, and Ronald Fagan (New York) has graciously helped with typing.

Finally, I would like to express my gratitude to Penelope for her tolerance and support during the many evenings and weekends I spent behind closed doors.

R. Paul Shaw
Population Division,
United Nations, N.Y.,
October, 1974

Northland College
Dexter Library
Ashland, WI 54806

Contents

1. Rural-Urban Population Redistribution in Latin America

ONE OF THE most important issues in the study of rural-urban population redistribution is the extent to which migration—aggregately conceptualized—is performing effectively as a mechanism for the redistribution of the economy's human resources. Effectiveness in this context can be gauged on the basis of two criteria. First, are rural-urban migrants behaving in the best interests of their short- and long-run perceived physical, social, and economic needs? As an adjunct, is migration, in fact, serving individual needs and interests well? Second, are rural-urban migrants behaving in the best interests of the economy as a whole, in terms of both its requirements for human-resource redistribution and the prospects and problems accompanying concentration or dispersion?

Relative to the first criterion, most surveys and cross-sectional studies of migration in developed and underdeveloped countries alike indicate that rural-urban migrants behave in an "economically rational" way or as "want satisfiers" in their pursuit of higher urban wages, better employment opportunities, and greater amenities (J. D. Tarver 1963, F. R. Oliver 1964, A. J. Fielding 1966, J. B. Lansing and E. Mueller 1967, B. Okun 1968, J. Vanderkamp 1968, J. C. Caldwell 1970, T. W. Rogers 1970, M. J. Greenwood and P. T. Gormerly 1971).[1] Often the concept of "push" and "pull" is adopted, whereby rural-urban migration is interpreted as reaction to un-

---

1. See R. P. Shaw (1974a) for a review of the literature.

desirable rural "pushes," desirable urban "pulls," or, most likely, a combination of the two (H. G. Karcel 1963, D. Winkleman 1964, S. Friedlander 1965, S. Taber 1968, G. L. Rutman 1970, M. McInnis 1971). If, as in many economic studies of migration, use is made of the cost-benefit framework, then migration behavior can also be interpreted as a form of personal investment where a decision to migrate from place i to j involves a calculation of higher returns to be gained by residing at place j (i.e., higher wages, less risk of unemployment) than costs to be incurred and opportunities forgone by leaving place i (L. A. Sjaastad 1961, 1962, M. J. Brennan 1965, W. D. Diehl 1966, H. J. Bodenjofer 1967, A. Speare, Jr. 1970). With respect to the migrant's utility calculus, then, it is reasonable to assume that in most rural-urban migration contexts, a positive value can be attached to voluntary decisions to migrate. That is, permanent rural-urban migration is not likely to take place unless this behavior actually results in greater fulfillment of the migrant's physical, social, and/or economic needs or unless he expects it to.

Evaluation of the second criterion, however—whether rural-urban migrants behave in the best interests of the economy—is much more difficult. On the one hand, we have the traditional view of rural-urban migration in the process of economic development. That is, rural-urban migration has typically been viewed analytically as a one-stage phenomenon in which a worker migrates from rural-agricultural activity of low productivity to a job of higher productivity in the urban-industrialized sector. A positive value is usually attached to this type of shift in accordance with the view that the transfer of a large proportion of workers from agricultural to industrial activity is highly correlated with economic development (W. A. Lewis 1955, H. B. Chenery 1960, B. Higgens 1967, J. Friedmann 1969). In fact, one of the best-known models of labor transfer and economic development has even proposed an intersectoral labor reallocation strategy as a means of simultaneously reducing surplus rural-agricultural labor (in the face of high rates of population growth) and channeling "unlimited supplies of cheap labor" into the urban-industrialized sector (J. Fei and G. Ranis 1964). (Needless to say, in many less-developed countries with high rates of rural and urban population increase, "cheap labor" is already in ample supply in large urban areas.)

On the other hand, as a number of studies indicate that not only the determinants but the direction and magnitude of rural-urban migration flows are likely to be time-and-place specific, it is not always possible to claim that rural-urban migration is conducive to balanced economic growth. For example, while rural in-migrants may create demands for locally produced urban goods and services and make possible rapid expansion of urban employment without strong upward pressures on urban wages, they may also add to problems of urban unemployment or underemployment and shortage of housing. At the same time, while rural out-migration may reduce rural unemployment by reducing competition for rural jobs, it may also lead to increasing rural unemployment due to the multiplier effect of migrants taking their consumer expenditures elsewhere. Another consideration is that if a rural area has both a competitive disadvantage in terms of the attractiveness of its labor market to populations of other rural or urban areas (i.e., wage and unemployment differentials) and a population heavily weighted with those who migrate readily (the young, best-educated, and, possibly, most productive or ambitious components of the origin population), then the growth of the rural area stands to be constrained on two counts (E. S. Lee *et al.* 1957, H. T. Eldridge and D. S. Thomas 1964). Finally, it is important to differentiate migration which appears to be in the interest of specific migrants from migration which runs counter to the national interest, in the sense that externalities such as high social costs attached to urban congestion and pollution may be inflicted on the social body.

An additional problem, and one addressed in this study, is that in certain cases, rural-urban migration flows may result in a misallocation of human resources relative to potentially productive natural resources.[2] From a national planning perspective, then, it may be important to divert, halt, or stimulate rural-urban migration flows (R. E. Beals and C. I. Menzes 1970, M. Miracle and L. Berry 1970, G. Olsson 1971). For example, in Latin America a number of rural-agricultural resettlement programs have been implemented to relocate "surplus agricultural labor" from seemingly overpopulated rural areas and to reduce strong rural-urban directional biases to particular urban "receiving areas." In the latter case, nonagricultural industries appear not to have been able to expand rapidly enough to contend with overcrowded labor markets; urban social overhead facilities such as housing, health services, and schooling have also fallen far behind social and economic welfare demands.

---

2. The implication, however, is not that the migrant is not maximizing his utilities. Rather, as noted previously, on the basis of the information available to him about actual opportunities elsewhere as opposed to actual opportunities at his current residence, his behavior is likely to be optimal toward fulfilling his wants.

TRENDS AND ISSUES IN LATIN AMERICAN MIGRATION

Over the last few decades, high rates of rural-urban migration in Latin America have led to a rapid transformation in the rural-urban population composition of most countries. In Table 1.1 estimates of rural-urban migration indicate net yearly rates as high as 2.8 percent over the 1950-60 decade. For most countries the influx of rural migrants to urban areas contributed up to 30-50 percent of the country's urban growth over the census interval.

As an illustration of the magnitudes of these intersectoral shifts in Latin America's population and labor force, consider the results of a "components of population and labor-force change technique" for Chile and Peru in Table 1.2.[3] In the case of Chile, approximately 22.8 out of every 100 rural population (Table 1.2, line G) migrated out of the rural sector over the 1952-60 period (or 2.85/100 per year). The corresponding figure for Peru (Table 1.2, line G) is approximately 34.0 per 100 over the period 1940-61 (or 1.62/100 per year). The significance of these rates in the growth of each country's urban sector is conveyed in line P, where approximately 36.9 percent of Chile's urban growth (1952-60) and 58.1 percent of Peru's urban growth (1940-61) can be attributed to an influx of rural migrants. In Colombia rural migrants also made a large contribution to the growth of the urban sector (36.5 percent) between 1951 and 1964, whereas migrants contributed only 19.8 percent of Costa Rica's urban growth over the period 1950-63. This difference will be explained in a later chapter.

In Table 1.3 estimates based on a study by Z. C. Camisa (1965) indicate average percentage increases in population size of cities due to migration (1950-60) ranging from 2 percent to 4 percent (line 1). Recognizing that the national rates of natural increase (line 3) represent only a crude indication of urban natural increase over the census interval (and, in this case, the rate of natural increase of specific cities), Camisa estimates (1) that total yearly increases in the size of these cities range from 3.6 percent for Argentina to 7.4 percent for Venezuela per decade, (2) that for Argentina and Venezuela, growth of city size due to in-migration exceeds that due to urban natural in-

---

3. In these estimates a two-sector model is used, since the urban and rural parts are largely equatable with industrial and agricultural economic activities, respectively.

In essence, the calculations in Table 1.2 are based upon a method for estimating components of intercensal labor-force and population changes. For a general idea of the type of data requirements, assumptions, and method utilized, see J. D. Durand and A. R. Miller (1969).

Table 1.1. Net Rural-Urban Migration--Selected Latin American Countries[a]

Country	Census Period	1[b]	2[c]	3[d]
Brazil	1950-60	3,334,271	10.0	1.0
Colombia	1951-64	1,777,200	28.6	2.2
Chile	1952-60	542,446	22.8	2.8
Ecuador	1950-62	518,716	18.3	1.5
El Salvador	1950-61	176,854	15.0	1.4
Mexico	1950-60	3,468,541	23.4	2.3
Paraguay	1950-62	235,402	27.3	2.3
Peru	1940-61	1,480,765	34.0	1.6
Costa Rica	1950-63	38,044	5.4	0.4

a. The basis for selecting these countries is that they demonstrate relatively high rates of rural-urban migration.

b. Net rural-urban migration over census period. Estimates based on vital statistics using average rates of natural increase from *United Nations Demographic Yearbooks* and population data from respective national censuses.

c. Estimated net rural-urban migration as a percentage of rural population at beginning of census period. Estimates based on vital statistics using average rates of natural increase from *United Nations Demographic Yearbooks* and population data from respective national censuses.

d. Average yearly intercensal rate of net rural-urban migration.

Table 1.2. Estimates of Population and Labor-Force Migration--Chile (1952-60) and Peru (1940-61)

	Chile	Peru
Rural Population Migration		
A. Rural population first census	2,380,000	4,357,105
B. Rural population second census	2,346,055	5,445,700
C. Average intercensal rural population (A + B/2)	2,368,177	4,901,403
D. National rate of natural increase per 100 per year (r)	24.5	22.3
E. Expected rural population second census in absence of migration (B x r) compounded annually for intercensal years n	2,888,501	7,021,582
F. Net rural population out-migration (E - B)	542,446	1,480,765
G. Net rural population out-migration per 100 rural population [F/(C/100)]	22.8	34.0
H. Net rate of population out-migration per year from rural sector (G/n)	2.8	1.6
Rural Labor-Force Migration		
I. % of male rural out-migrants	0.475	0.492
J. Rural male crude activity rates over intercensal period	0.559	0.495
K. Rural labor-force out-migrants (F x I x J)	144,033	360,625
L. Net rate of male labor-force out-migration per year from rural sector (H x I x J)	0.74	0.39

Urban Population Growth Due to Rural In-Migrants

M.	Urban population first census	3,561,450	2,323,420
N.	Urban population second census	5,028,060	4,873,800
O.	Intercensal urban population growth	1,466,610	2,550,380
P.	Approximate % of intercensal urban population growth due to rural in-migrants (F/O)	36.9	58.1

Notes: (1) The annual population growth rate indicated by the censuses (including net international migration) is 2.5 percent for both Chile and Peru. For Chile, then, our calculations using the rate of natural increase (lines D through H) appear to correspond closely with the census growth rates. For Peru, however, there is an appreciable discrepancy, which suggests the possibility of the birth and death data understating the true rate of natural increase. The rate of 25/1,000 suggested by the census may well be a better estimate. On that basis, the estimate of net rural out-migration would be increased by about 175,000 for Peru. The annual net out-migration rate would be about 1.8 percent (not 1.6 percent). The percentage urban growth due to migration would rise to about 65 percent.

(2) It is important to point out a number of factors which may affect the accuracy of an estimate of net migration as a residual (line F). First, rural population counts for both the first and second censuses may be either over- or underenumerated. Second, the rate of natural increase may be in error due to underregistration or internal migration into rural areas. Finally, it should be noted that urban re-classification and annexation are not included.

(3) The same qualifications in note 2 apply to our estimate of rural labor-force out-migration (line K) with the addition that some error may be introduced by our means of calculating the proportion of rural out-migrants that are males. Possible errors are noted in Appendix II.

(4) It should be noted that our estimate of intercensal urban population growth due to in-migration (line P) implies a natural increase in Peru's urban population at about the same rate as the 2.2 percent for total and rural population. However, if the total and rural natural increase rate is raised to 2.5 percent, as suggested by the census estimate (note 1), the urban natural increase rate will be reduced to about 1.6 percent.

crease, and (3) that the influx of in-migrants (not necessarily rural in-migrants) contributed from 42 to 54 percent of the growth in these cities over the decade.[4]

As for the characteristics of the migrants themselves, most studies indicate that Latin American migration is selective for those in the ages 15-24, the single, females over males, and the highly educated, and that the principal motive for migration is economic or "work-related," with the majority of the rural-urban migrants "first-employment seekers," farmers, and unskilled workers (J. Elizaga n.d., B. Herrick 1965, D. W. Adams 1969, W. Flinn and D. Cartano 1970). As an illustration of the age-sex distribution of migrants in two countries with very different patterns of rural-urban migration, Table 1.4 provides estimates of intercensal rural-urban cohort migration for Chile and Costa Rica.[5]

Now, are rural-urban migrants in Latin America behaving in the best interests of their short- and long-run perceived physical, social, and economic needs? If decisions to migrate in Latin America are voluntary—as they usually are—and urban movements are relatively permanent (i.e., presuming the option of return migration is open), then the answer is a highly probable "yes."[6] Again, survey and cross-sectional studies of migration in Latin America support this view (B. Herrick 1965, J. Elizaga 1966, G. S. Sahota 1968, D. W. Adams 1969, H. L. Browning and W. Feindt 1969, E. W. Block and S. Iutaka 1969).

Is rural-urban migration behaving in the best interests of the economies of Latin America in terms of their requirements for human resource redistribution and prospects and problems accom-

4. Camisa's estimates of the impact of in-migration on the growth of Latin America's largest cities may not be entirely representative of the experience of smaller urban centers, given the obvious directional biases in Latin American migration to single urban "receiving areas."

5. Clearly, in both countries migration is more selective with respect to females. A peculiarity, however, is that even though rates of female rural-urban migration fall off considerably faster than do rates of male rural-urban migration in each country, they also pick up after the ages of 40-44 in Chile and 35-44 in Costa Rica. Only for male rural-urban migrants in Chile are we able to claim that the general principle holds of migration selectivity in the ages 15-29 with a tapering-off thereafter. Of course, age-specific error factors may be a possible explanation of the erratic age patterns of the rates, though for both Chile and Costa Rica age data were smoothed before calculating the rates.

One explanation for the predominance of females in Latin American rural-urban migration has been hypothesized by Herrick (1965) in his study of migration in Chile. Herrick argues that, in the face of high rates of rural population growth, the number of workers offering to supply their labor services exceeds the number demanded by employers; excess supply is particularly problematic among fresh additions to the labor force, that is, males and females arriving at economically active

Table 1.3. Migration to Five Latin American Clusters

	Greater Buenos Aires (Argentina)		Federal District of Mexico (Mexico)		Metropolitan Area of Caracas (Venezuela)		City of Panamá (Panama)		City of Guayaquil (Ecuador)	
Line 1[a] (average % yearly increase of city size due to migration 1950-60[b])										
	M	F	M	F	M	F	M	F	M	F
	2.1	2.1	2.0	1.9	4.0	3.9	1.5	2.2	2.8	3.1
Line 2 (% of each country's total population in the above cities[c])										
	1960		1963		1964		1964		1960	
	32.1		8.9		21.1		29.6		11.0	
Line 3 (rates of national natural increase, 1950-60 averaged[d])										
	1.53		3.40		3.42		2.04		3.05	

a. Male and female city population aged 10-60 years.

b. Z. C. Camisa (1965, pp. 408-11).

c. United Nations Statistical Bulletin for Latin America, 1965.

d. United Nations Demographic Yearbooks.

Table 1.4. Intercensal Rural-Urban Cohort Migration in Chile and Costa Rica (1950-63)[a]

Age Cohorts		Males				Females			
1950	1960	1[b]	2[c]	3[d]	4[e]	1[b]	2[c]	3[d]	4[e]
Chile									
5-9	15-19	176,500	126,500	50,000	28.3	171,600	101,600	70,000	47.9
10-14	20-24	144,500	99,700	44,800	31.0	141,900	80,300	61,700	43.6
15-19	25-29	126,800	79,700	47,100	37.0	105,500	67,500	38,000	35.9
20-24	30-34	102,100	74,400	27,700	27.1	88,700	62,400	26,300	29.9
25-29	35-39	80,200	62,100	18,100	22.5	72,500	54,900	17,600	24.3
30-34	40-44	72,100	57,400	14,700	20.6	66,800	47,800	19,000	24.3
35-39	45-49	64,900	53,200	11,700	18.0	58,400	44,300	14,100	25.8
40-44	50-54	60,300	47,100	13,200	21.9	51,300	37,200	14,100	27.5
45-49	55-59	44,800	36,400	8,400	18.7	41,000	29,300	11,700	28.5
50-54	60-64	38,700	31,800	6,900	17.8	35,300	26,300	9,000	28.3
Costa Rica[f]									
5-9	18-22	39,800[g]	37,500[g]	2,300	5.8	40,600[g]	34,000[g]	6,600	16.3
10-14	23-27	32,600	31,000	1,600	5.3	33,800	29,500	4,300	12.6
15-24	28-37	51,300	48,800	2,500	5.0	47,200	46,200	1,000	2.1
25-34	38-47	35,900	34,800	1,100	3.0	32,200	30,900	1,300	4.0
35-44	48-57	25,800	25,100	700	2.6	22,600	21,100	1,500	6.5
45-54	58-67	14,900	14,800	100	0.8	13,200	12,200	1,000	7.1
55-64	68-77	7,100	6,900	200	3.0	6,000	5,600	400	7.5
65+	78+	3,100	3,000	100	2.5	2,700	2,600	100	5.0

a. In this table, rates of rural out-migration are calculated using a cohort method. In Table 1.2, rates of rural out-migration were calculated using rates of natural increase and projection techniques. In the case of Chile, a comparison of the two estimates can be made. In Table 1.2, then, we estimated 542,446 net rural out-migrants for the period 1952–60. Extending the period from 1952–60 to 1950–60 would, of course, result in a larger estimate. In Table 1.4 we estimated approximately 522,000 rural out-migrants (that is, the sum of column 3 for males and column 3 for females) for the period 1950–60. This estimate would also be considerably larger had we been able to account for the migration of approximately 340,000 children aged 0–4 years from 1955–60 and approximately 102,000 aged 65 years and over. Generally, then, there appears to be a fairly good correspondence between the results of the two methods.

b. Expected rural cohort population 1960. The estimates in column 1 were taken from the "components of intercensal population and labor-force change technique," applied to Chile for 1950–60. The procedure is illustrated in Appendix I for a population cohort.

c. Enumerated rural cohort population 1960.

d. Number of cohort rural–urban migrants 1950–60 (column 2 – column 1).

e. Cohort rural–urban migrants as % of 1960 expected cohort population (3/1).

f. These estimates were prepared by the Population Division of the United Nations in a study entitled "An Analytic Study of the Urban and Rural Population of Costa Rica," Working Paper No. 22, Nov. 1967, 67–49702.

g. Columns 1 and 2 for Costa Rica indicate figures for 1963.

panying concentration? Although few, if any, studies of rural-urban migration in Latin America have posed the question in just this way, a number of studies concerned with the process of population redistribution and economic development indicate that for many countries, the answer may be "no." For example, in a study of rural-urban migration in Chile, B. Herrick (1965, p. 2) points out:

> We can, however, suggest a model in which the urban migrant is not such a clear sign of well-being in the economy. The value of a worker's output in agriculture, instead of improving over time, may actually stagnate or decline as a result of outmoded land-tenure arrangements, excessive division of land parcels, backwardness of the cultivators, unfavorable terms of trade, or other disincentive factors. Rural poverty may thus force young laborers, the children of farm families, into the cities to look for work. These migrants, sometimes lacking in education or occupational skills, may only be able to drift into tiny handicraft shops, unskilled work in construction, or personal services, rather than find employment in a growing modern industrial sector.
>
> Thus, the signs of economic development—urban migration accompanied by expanding secondary and tertiary sectors and relatively contracting primary ones—are seen. But development, here thought of as "industrialization"—the growth within the economies of technological advantage, high-productive activities—is not occurring. Failure of incomes to grow may be only one manifestation of this frustrated shift in the industrial distribution of the labor force without corresponding economic growth. . . . The vociferous demands for social services by the new urban agglomerations will bump against the country's financial ability to provide these services, since increases in governmental spending power may be hampered by

---

ages. As rural employment opportunities are believed to be in particularly short supply for females and as the demand for female domestic workers has been on the upswing in urban areas, it has been argued that these factors have led to particularly high rates of rural out-migration for the young, unmarried female. National census data on rural-urban differentials in female labor-force participation rates support this view. For example, in Chile and Costa Rica, while urban and rural male activity rates are approximately equal (they are actually slightly higher in rural areas), urban female activity rates are, on the average, three to four times as high as rural female activity rates. Acknowledging census definitional problems in measuring female labor-force participation rates, it seems safe to assume that the ratio of urban to rural female activity rates is at least 2:1. Also, females employed in urban areas are overwhelmingly concentrated in the young, unmarried category with the implication that work-seeking rural female migrants have added to this pool.

6. Involuntary migration would consist of forced or impelled migration.

the failure of the economy to place the new workers in more productive occupations.

L. J. Ducoff (1965, p. 203) makes a similar point in his study of the role of migration in the demographic development of Latin America as a whole:

> While, normally, the role of migration is the achievement of a better distribution of population in relation to resources and economic opportunities, the effectiveness of such a redistribution is always related to the absorptive capacities of the areas receiving the migration streams. In Latin America, the rate and volume of rural-urban migration far exceed the current absorptive capacities of the principal cities, thus creating widespread underemployment and serious housing, education, and other social problems.

In a study of internal migration in Brazil, E. Fischlowitz (1968, p. 41) argues that government passivity with respect to conditions in the rural sector is somewhat responsible for a misallocation of resources.

> Unfortunately the official attitude of the Brazilian government toward internal migration can be characterized with only slight exaggeration, as that of an ostrich. Practically speaking, almost nothing was or is being done to orient the chaotic flow of displaced persons, to make better use of idle human resources, or, at least, to attenuate their distressing social conditions by means of adequate labor exchanges, assistance, and related measures.

And in a projection of agricultural and nonagricultural growth rates required to absorb new entries to the labor forces of Costa Rica and El Salvador, J. B. Gordon (1969, p. 319) points out that, in the face of high population growth rates, "often the planner is caught between giving the country's population a choice between continued rural underemployment or unemployment in some hovel on the fringe of some urban center."

There seems to be some consensus, then, that current magnitudes of rural-urban population redistribution have not been beneficial to the urban "receiving areas." In fact, development planners have expressed considerable concern over high rates of in-migration resulting in increasing rates of urban unemployment, underemployment in the service sector, concentration of rural in-migrants in

Table 1.5. Select Data on Urban Unemployment and Extent of Urban Slums

Part A

Country	Province or Region	City	Period	% of Labor Force	% Unemployed	% of Employed Working Less Than 35 Hrs.
Chile[a]	Santiago	Gran Santiago	1952 (June)		4.6	
			1958		8.0	
			1959 (Jan + Mar)		8.9	
			1960		7.5	10.5
	Valparaíso	Valparaíso + Viña del Mar	1952		4.6	
			1958 (June)		7.0	
			1959 (Jan + Mar)		8.3	
			1960 (June)		7.6	17.0
	Coquimbo	La Serena	1952		3.2	
			1960 (Sep)		8.3	
		La Serena + Coquimbo	1960 (Dec)		11.2	10.4
	Antofagasta	Antofagasta	1952		4.8	
			1960 (Dec + Sep)		9.0	11.3
	Tarapaca	Iquique	1952		8.6	
			1960 (Dec)		9.1	
			1961 (Mar + Sep)			8.7
	Valdivia	Valdivia	1952		11.1	
			1960 (Mar + Sep)		9.8	
			1961			7.0

Concepción	Concepción + Talcahuano	1968		10.9	16.0
		1969		11.0	14.0
Concepción	Coronel + Lota	1968		15.3	12.6
		1969		15.2	10.0
Colombia[b]					
	Urban visible unemployment	1967	14		
	Urban disguised unemployment		7		
	Urban visible underemployment		2		
	Urban disguised underemployment		3		
Colombia[c]	Bogotá	1968			
	Males aged 15-24		41		
	Males aged 15+		26		
Colombia[d]	Atlántico	1972		14	
	Underemployment		7		
	Oriental	1972		8	
	Underemployment		5		
	Bogotá	1972		7	
	Underemployment		13		
	Central	1972		13	
	Underemployment		19		

Country	Province or Region	City	Period	% of Labor Force	% Unemployed	% of Employed Working Less Than 35 Hrs.
	Pacífica Underemployment		1972	13	11	
Colombia[d]		Bogotá	1971-72		8	
		Barranquilla	1971-72		12	
		Cartagena	1971-72		11	
		Bucaramanga	1971-72		6	
		Cúcuta	1971-72		9	
		Medellín	1971-72		13	
		Cali	1971-72		12	
		Manizales	1971-72		14	
Venezuela[b]		Caracas Visible unemployment	1961-67	17		
Panama[c]			1963-64			
	Males aged 15-24			18		
	Males aged 15+			9		
Trinidad and Tobago[c]			1968			
	Males aged 15-24			26		
	Males aged 15+			14		

Part B: Extent of Urban Slums and Uncontrolled Settlements[e]

Country	City	Period	Slums and Uncontrolled Settlements as % of City Population
Brazil	Rio de Janeiro	1947	20
	Rio de Janeiro	1961	27
	Brasília	1962	41
	São Paulo	1960-67	47
Chile	Santiago	1964	25
Colombia	Cali	1964	30
	Buenaventura	1964	80
Mexico	México City	1952	14
	México City	1966	46
Peru	Lima	1957	9
	Lima	1969	36
Venezuela	Caracas	1960	21
	Caracas	1970	40
	Maracaibo	1960	50

a. Banco Central de Chile, *Boletín Mensual*, 1962-70.

b. International Labour Office, Country Studies.

c. D. Turnham, *The Employment Problem in LDC's*, OECD, Paris, 1971.

d. United Nations Population Files.

e. United Nations Center for Housing and Planning.

politically volatile shanty towns, and "overurbanization."[7] This is particularly evident in recent national-development plans and statements by a number of Latin American governments attending the 1974 World Population Conference. For example, governments perceiving rates of growth of their metropolitan regions as excessive (i.e., intervention-desirable) include Argentina, Chile, Colombia, Dominican Republic, Ecuador, Guyana, Jamaica, Cuba, Mexico, Nicaragua, Panama, Peru, Uruguay, and Venezuela.

Although data on rates of urban unemployment in Latin America are both scanty and often questionable, rates for Chile and Colombia in Table 1.5, part A, clearly indicate excess supply in the face of high rates of in-migration. Also, consider the following developments within the Chilean economy over the 1952-60 period, during which Chile's urban sector grew by approximately 30 percent due to rural-urban migration:

1. The visible nonagricultural unemployment level was, on the average, three times that of the agricultural unemployment level in Chile's twenty-five provinces, and real wages in the urban sector dropped by approximately 8 percent, due possibly to the influx of unskilled in-migrants (F. S. Weaver 1968).

2. Urban unemployment at least doubled in every major Chilean city (from 4 to 8 percent); underemployment rose considerably (that is, approximately 12 percent of Chile's labor force was working less than thirty-five hours per week).

3. Rates of intraprovincial rural-urban migration were highly associated (curvilinearly) with declines in provincial urban activity rates, again indicating possible increases in disguised unemployment.

4. The majority of urban in-migrants from rural areas were absorbed into the service industry, whereas the service industry's contribution to the country's gross domestic product did not increase.

5. The estimated 1960 housing deficiency in Chile's urban sector of each province was, on the average, five times that of the rural sector, ranging from a deficiency of 18.5/100 in the province of Valparaíso to 56.8/100 in the province of Linares (*Antecedentes Básicos* 1964).

It would be difficult to argue that the trends described in numbers 4 and 5 are unique to Chile; serious housing shortages (see Table 1.5, part B) and disguised unemployment in services characterize a large majority of Latin American urban centers.

7. The implication, however, is not that in-migrants alone are the urban unemployed. Rather, it is their addition to the total urban labor force which results in an excess supply.

Unfortunately, few development planners view the rural "sending areas" as being able to accommodate the expanding population base (as an exception see W. C. Thiesenhusen 1969). Rather, as large numbers have migrated out of rural areas, planners have been quick to infer that both actual and potential income-earning possibilities must be inadequate—especially relative to opportunities in the cities. A foregone conclusion of this type of interpretation is that the possibility of "underruralization" is largely ruled out. Consequently a great deal of attention has been focused on Latin America's urban areas as necessary "receiving areas" and on the efforts required to overcome the innumerable economic, social, psychological, ecological, and political problems of accommodation. For example, a recent Ford Foundation report (1971) on rural-urban migration in Chile adopts the view that the influx of rural migrants is essentially a phenomenon which must be "adjusted for" by providing more urban jobs and housing, and by allocating scarce social overhead capital funds to urban areas.

Not surprisingly, the view above is in keeping with the position that as urbanization is usually associated with industrialization, and nonagricultural industry is usually associated with economic development, then the bulk of the developmental effort in Latin America should be directed toward devising and implementing new forms of nonagricultural technology and urban expansion (J. Friedmann 1967, 1969). A concomitant of this approach is that the urban sector will inevitably demonstrate a consistent advantage over the rural sector with respect to wage levels and amenities. In fact, since enforcement of higher legal wages, housing standards, etc., is likely to be more effective in urban areas than in rural areas, the comparative advantage of the urban sector is almost guaranteed. As suggested by M. P. Todaro (1969) and J. R. Harris and M. P. Todaro (1970), it should not be surprising that rural-urban migration, in the face of high rates of unemployment, may still appear "economically rational" if a great disparity between urban and rural income-producing possibilities increases the mathematical expectation of urban wages to a level where it is more advantageous to risk temporary unemployment in the city than to opt for the certainty of a low-subsistence rural income.

PROSPECTS OF "UNDERRURALIZATION" IN LATIN AMERICA

In proposing that a number of Latin America's economies may be "underruralized," I am running against the empirical tide. For example, qualitative and statistical studies suggest that agriculture in many Latin American countries is in a slow growth state and that rates of growth of agricultural output have fallen behind rates of total rural-population growth. As an indication of the poor performance of agriculture in three countries, estimates in Table 1.6 suggest annual deficits in agricultural production relative to demand ranging from −0.3 for Costa Rica to −1.0 for Peru. The situation is similar in the Dominican Republic, El Salvador, Honduras, Jamaica, Panama, Argentina, Bolivia, Brazil, Colombia, Paraguay, and Uruguay.

Now, if the actual levels of rural wages, unemployment, and amenities are considered inferior to those in the urban sector and if they are taken to be representative of the potential rural level of living standards, then, indeed, it may be that rural-urban migration should be viewed as a necessary means of alleviating rural labor supply-demand disequilibrium and accompanying disparities in rural-urban labor productivity and wage levels. The question, however, is whether actual income-producing possibilities in rural Latin America are representative of potential income-producing possibilities.[8] Does the disparity between the rate of growth of per capita agricultural output and population growth accurately reflect the capacity of Latin American agriculture to absorb increasing supplies of "labor on the land"? In other terms, is the widening of income and amenity differentials due to a more rapid rise in urban incomes, or is it due also to rural income and welfare levels being "held back"?

This study argues that a considerable divergence exists between actual and potential agricultural income-producing possibilities in the majority of Latin America's economies. One consideration is that government price policies have tended to favor the urban consumer or have attempted to fight national inflation through controls designed to hold down the cost of such basic food items as meat, milk, bread, and vegetables. As the dominant reason, however, this study focuses on the organization of productive activity (i.e., institutions and policies) as the major impediment to the effective use of potentially productive labor and nonlabor agricultural resources. The author's position is that the organization of productive activity in Latin American agriculture (in combination with high rates of population growth) is operating as the major stimulus to rural out-migration and as the major cause of a misallocation of human

8. "Potential income-producing possibilities" do not include future use of typically nonagricultural resources, but means of rural-agricultural production utilizing potential arable or pasture land without extensive frontier development.

Table 1.6. Indexes of Agricultural Performance in Costa Rica, Chile, and Peru (1952-68)[a]

	Costa Rica	Chile	Peru	Colombia
A. Average compound annual growth rate of agricultural production[b]	4.2	2.1	3.1	3.3
B. Average compound annual growth rate of agricultural domestic demand[b]	4.5	3.0	4.1	3.9
C. Average compound annual growth rate of deficit or surplus in production relative to demand (A − B)	−0.3	−0.9	−1.0	−0.6
Indexes of per capita production for 1964-66 (1954-56 = 100)				
Crops	115	101	103	101
Livestock products	64	85	106	101
Food	86	94	100	101
Total	100	91	103	101
Average % of economically active population employed in agriculture				
Total	49.2	27.5	49.8	48.9
Male	57.7	34.1	54.8	59.5
Female	5.4	4.3	31.7	12.4

a. Source: U. S. Department of Agriculture, no. 257, Tables 1-6.

b. The compound annual growth rate in agricultural domestic demand equals the compound annual growth rate of population and the compound annual growth rate in per capita real income times the coefficient of income elasticity. Coefficients of income elasticity of demand for agricultural products are assumed (in the above-quoted study) to vary with per capita income per year as follows: less than $200 = 0.7, $200-$400 = 0.5, $600+ = 0.3.

resources away from potentially productive agricultural areas. Thus, rather than address "effects" or "symptoms" to which potential rural migrants are likely to respond (such as rural wage and unemployment differentials), this study seeks to identify the "causes" underlying such "effects." In so doing, it relates to important planning and policy concerns such as: "What measures would have to be taken to stimulate, divert, or halt rural-urban migration flows in specific countries if it were deemed necessary? Are large rural-urban migration flows in Latin America phenomena which must merely be 'adjusted for' while attempting to cope with such problems as urban housing shortages and increasing rates of national unemployment and underemployment? Is the 'mechanism' of rural-urban migration in Latin America operating effectively in its allocation of the economy's population and labor force relative to actual opportunities in the country's urban sector and potentially productive resources in the country's rural sector?"

MEANS OF EVALUATION

The preceding proposition requires both development of a theoretical framework and empirical verification. A first task is to describe the nature of productive activity in Latin American agriculture. Next a model is presented which addresses agricultural income-producing possibilities, possible situations of economic stress in the face of high rates of natural increase, and rural out-migration as a reaction to situations of economic stress. The crux of the model is that "institutional factors" in Latin American agriculture typically operate to impede effective utilization of labor and nonlabor agricultural resources and that, in the face of a high and increasing stock and flow of labor supply, situations of economic stress evolve rapidly. The "institution" of central importance is the system of land tenure. Those likely to experience the greatest difficulty in meeting level-of-living requirements (the minifundio and landless employee class) are those predicted to demonstrate the greatest propensity to migrate to urban areas offering seemingly better opportunities.

The second task of this study is to evaluate the relationship between empirical measures of agricultural inopportunity or economic stress and measures of rural out-migration. In this endeavor an attempt will be made to evaluate the relative importance of the organization of productive activity in agriculture as a causal factor in rural-urban migration, by considering also the importance of rural-urban differentials in levels of living and amenities. While rural-urban differentials cannot be assumed to be independent of the organization of productive activity in agriculture, their relationship to migration, in contrast to their relationship to agricultural organization per se, should permit some separation of rural "pushes" and urban "pulls" in migration.

Finally, this study attempts to evaluate whether changes in the organization of productive activity in Latin American agriculture are likely to result in more efficient utilization of potentially productive agricultural resources and/or higher rates of growth of per capita agricultural output. A key planning or policy concern in this discussion is whether or not efforts could be made toward clotting rural out-migration. Such a strategy would only seem reasonable, however, if the evidence suggested that specific Latin American countries are indeed "underruralized." That is, at a minimum, this study will have to suggest that prospects exist for more efficient agricultural resource use and that inefficient resource use has been, in itself, an important influence in rural out-migration.

One shortcoming of this study is that it is somewhat one-sided. That is, its focus is largely on prospects of "underruralization" and on the "whos," "wheres," and "whys" of the rural "pushes" in Latin American rural-urban migration, rather than the urban "pulls." This means that the important issue of whether rural-urban migration has actually been detrimental to the development of urban economies in Latin America over the last few decades is not tackled. At most, this study will proceed on the assurance that contemporary rural-urban migration flows have come to constitute a burden on areas such as urban labor and housing markets.

ORGANIZATION

In the following chapter, a model of the determinants of rural out-migration in Latin America is formulated. Drawing on both qualitative and quantitative sources, a number of assumptions are generated about productive organization and activity within the minifundio-latifundio complex. These assumptions lay the foundation for a theoretical model of income-producing possibilities, likely situations of economic stress for the majority of Latin America's rural-agricultural population and labor force, and out-migration as a response. In Chapter 3 means of testing the empirical relevance of the model are presented, and hypotheses are stated. The units of analysis for the empirical tests consist of migration at the provincial level for Chile, Peru, Colombia, and Costa Rica and the migration experience of a number of Latin American economies at the national level. Both within- and between-country analyses are performed. Chapter 4 presents empirical findings based largely on correlation and multiple-regression analysis. Chapter 5 considers the likelihood of increasing production possibilities (i.e., decreasing situations of economic stress) through changes in the nature of productive activity and, consequently, the likelihood of clotting rural out-migration. Chapter 6 presents a summary and conclusions.

2. Theoretical Model

T HIS CHAPTER details a model of determinants of out-
migration from the rural-agricultural sectors of a number of
Latin American economies.[1] Essentially, the model is economically
deterministic.[2] Income-producing possibilities of the rural-
agricultural labor force and subsequently the extent to which minifundio, landless employee/tenant, intermediate-sized farm, and latifundio households are able to fulfill living-level requirements and
aspirations, are interpreted primarily as a function of agricultural
production and wage-earning possibilities within the minifundio-

1. In most Latin American economies, the rural and urban sectors can be equated
largely with agricultural and industrial production, respectively. In this discussion,
"rural" and "agricultural" are used interchangeably, implying that the model will be
limited (at least for purposes of testing) to those Latin American economies in which
the majority of the rural labor force (e.g., 80 percent) is economically active in
agricultural occupations in the agricultural industry.

2. Is an economically deterministic model theoretically justified? While migration
theory tells us that economic considerations are of major importance in explaining
geographic labor mobility, it is also important to recognize that noneconomic considerations such as information flows, availability of transportation, geographical
barriers, the effect of friends and relatives, differential amenities, inertia, and housing tenure are also important in accounting for migration in general and for the
behavior of specific subgroups. However, moving from the context of the developed
to the underdeveloped countries, empirical studies suggest that the economic motive
dominates (R.P. Shaw 1974a, chap. 4). Accordingly, as this study will argue that the
majority of the rural-agricultural population in a number of Latin American economies is merely striving to maintain living-level requirements, our position will be
that such factors as differential amenities and desired proximity to friends and relatives play a much weaker role as "conditioners" in the decision to migrate than
purely economic considerations. Of course, this view should and will be subjected to
empirical inquiry.

latifundio complex.[3] Where conditions of less-than-satisfactory agricultural participation emerge, high rates of population and labor-force out-migration (largely to urban areas offering greater opportunities) are interpreted as a response.[4]

The model applies to Latin American economies with high and increasing rates of natural increase and in which the structure of land tenure can be characterized by a large proportion of the rural-agricultural population centralized on minifundios and a large proportion of the agricultural land held by latifundistas. Exemplary countries and data indicating polar extremes in the distribution of land are listed in Table 2.1.

Crucial to the development of the model are a number of assumptions about the effect of the "institutional context and structure" of Latin America's land tenure system on (1) agricultural production possibilities, (2) the efficiency of the distribution of rural-agricultural labor to land resources, and, (3) subsequently, employment opportunities in the rural-agricultural sector. An important premise is that the distribution of labor to nonlabor resources (essentially land) in the rural-agricultural sector is institutionally rigid and that accompanying "institutional arrangements" have conditioned the cost of land, its use, availability, and development to the extent that social and economic opportunities for minifundio owners and the landless employee/tenant class have been stifled. In combination with (1) increasing dependency ratios among minifundio farm and landless employee families (due to high fertility and falling infant and childhood mortality), and (2) fresh additions to both the minifundio farm-family labor force and the landless employee/tenant work force, it is argued that a higher ratio of population and labor force to *available land* has resulted. Consequently, out-migration—conceptualized either aggregately as a "population pressure escape valve" or subjectively as "economically rational behavior in the face of economic adversity"—is interpreted as a response.

As a number of assumptions are made concerning the nature of productive activity in the minifundio-latifundio complex, it is important to bring empirical evidence to bear on this subject. Before formulating the model, then, let us turn to a description of the

3. For this study, a minifundio is defined as a farm holding less than 5 hectares in size. A latifundio (operated by a latifundista) is defined as a farm holding in excess of 500 hectares. The latifundio class will be referred to as *latifundismo*.

4. That is, "satisfactory" in terms of the hours a worker would like to work, although he may be inhibited from doing so, toward meeting subsistence requirements, or given aspirations and/or utility profile attached to his marginal valuation of labor as against returns obtainable.

Table 2.1. Proportion of the National Labor Force in Agricultural Occupations, Distribution of Holdings and Land by Farm Size, and Rates of Population Growth for Selected Latin American Countries (1950-65)

Country	Year	% of National Labor Force in Agricultural Occupations[a]	Minifundios		Latifundios		1950-60 Rates of Population Growth[c]
			% of Farms <5 Hectares	% of Ag. Land[b]	% of Farms >500 Hectares	% of Ag. Land[b]	
Costa Rica	1955[d]	48	44.4	3.1	0.5	33.0	4.0
Brazil	1960[e]	48	44.8	2.4	0.9	44.2	2.1
Colombia	1960	43	62.5	4.5	0.7	40.5	3.1
Chile	1965	24	49.8	0.7	2.5	79.8	2.5
Ecuador	1954	52	73.1	7.2	0.4	45.0	3.0
El Salvador	1961	59	83.5	5.7	0.1	23.8	3.5
Mexico	1960	52	65.9	0.8	2.7	84.6	3.5
Paraguay	1961	50	45.4		1.4	88.7	3.5
Peru	1961	47	83.5	5.8	0.4	75.0	3.0
Bolivia	1950	65	59.3	0.2	7.9	95.1	2.3

a. *Food and Agricultural Organization Yearbook*, vol. 20 (1966).

b. Pan American Union, *América en cifras, situación económica: I agricultura, ganadería.*

c. *United Nations Demographic Yearbook*, 1950-64.

d. Size distribution of farms given for less than 7 hectares (not 5) and greater than 700 hectares (not 500).

e. Size distribution of farms given for less than 10 hectares (not 5) and greater than 1,000 hectares (not 500).

nature of productive activity within the "institutional context and structure" of land tenure in Latin American agriculture.

The Organization of Productive Activity in Latin American Agriculture

Within the minifundio-latifundio complex, productive activity can be allocated along a continuum beginning with subsistence-production family farms utilizing family labor only, to large-scale production farms utilizing substantial amounts of salaried and wage labor. The range of income-producing possibilities for the rural-agricultural labor force lies in either one or some combination of the following:

1. Operation of one's own land, e.g., by the family head and unpaid family labor;

2. Operation of rented land on a sharecropping or fixed-rent basis, e.g., as a resident tenant or on a seasonal or occasional basis;

3. Work as a farm employee, e.g., as a resident or seasonal employee;

4. Nonfarm work, e.g., in a close-by urban location or as a domestic on a latifundio.

Of course, opportunities within the first three possibilities will depend on a number of economic and social factors determining

1. Land productivity, e.g., land quality, weather;

2. Price of land for expansion of production and prices of nonland inputs relative to value of output;

3. Shifts in the production function, e.g., technological change, availability of credit for financing new nonlabor inputs, better education of the labor force;

4. Efficiency of the market mechanism;

5. Possibilities of employment on someone else's land.

On the other hand, off-farm work will depend largely on the proximity of the agricultural worker to alternative nonfarm employment opportunities.

How can the above possibilities—and opportunities within each—be characterized in Latin American agriculture? To address this question, a number of studies have been catalogued which investigate conditions playing an important role in productive activity in Latin American agriculture. Consider Table 2.2. Although this approach is less favorable than a more detailed review of the findings, limitations in methodology, etc., of each study, it has been chosen in the interests of brevity. Now, it is important to state a

Table 2-2: Conditions in Latin American Agriculture

Conditions	Support	Comments
Structure of Land Tenure is Institutionally Rigid and the Distribution of Income is Unequal	E. Feder (1964), CIDA (1966; Peru, Colombia, Chile, Argentina, Brazil, Guatemala, Ecuador), A.R. Holmberg et.al. (1969), T.L. Smith (1967;Colombia), S. Barraclough (1970)	Where agrarian reforms have been in effect, their progress has been slow. That the structure of land tenure is relatively constant is revealed in comparisons of census farm distributions by size over the last few decades. In most cases, cost of land is beyond the means of minifundio owners or of the landless working class. When land is expropriated from latifundistas, they manage to reestablish the size of their holdings through new land purchases. Incentives to migrate to new land settlements are often stifled as upon settlement and initial clearing, latifundistas are likely to arrive and expel occupants. According to CIDA (1966) estimates, the (a) average land area of a latifundio as a multiple of average land area of a minifundio and (b) average income per latifundio as a multiple of average income per minifundio are in the following magnitudes respectively; Argentine, 270 & 66; Brazil, 546 & 62; Chile, 1549 & 72; Colombia, 491 & 36; Ecuador, 618 & 165; Guatemala, 1732 & 499.
Technology, Land and Labor Quality are Relatively Fixed on Minifundios	CIDA (1966), FAO–IBRD (1959; Peru), L.T. Smith (1967; Colombia), P.R. Crosson (1970; Chile), R.G. Paulston (1971;Peru)	CIDA reports that a general trend in countries such as Brazil, Ecuador, Peru and Guatemala is that minifundio sizes are actually decreasing from an average of 2.6 to 2.4 hectares. Land is costly and institutional forces are cited as inhibiting social and economic vertical mobility via the acquisition of land – especially by means of controlling credit. For example, the FAO–IBRD study reports that good land in the department of Arequipa, Peru costs an average of 40,000 soles per hectare while the average field worker earns 10.25 soles per day (or approximately 2000 per 200 work day year). Also, parcelling of land due to inheritance rights is cited as a significant problem for the distribution of water, arranging drainage and introducing technology. Also for Peru, it was reported that one third of the minifundios are hand cultivated, that non-land and non-labor inputs are too costly relative to the value of output and that high interest rates inhibit producers from utilizing new inputs such as fertilizers. A concomitant of the more or less rigid social and economic structure is that the peasantry has limited access to either formal or technological schooling.

Conditions	Support	Comments
The Land Tenure System, Credit Possibilities and Pricing and Marketing Arrangements Impede Possibilities of Higher Incomes on Minifundios	E. Feder (1964), T.W. Schultz (1966), W.C. Thiesenhusen (1967;Chile), T.L. Smith (1967;Colombia), J.R. Riberio et.al. (1969;Brazil), D. F. Fienup et.al. (1969; Argentina), E. Haney (1969; Colombia), W.R. Cline (1970; Chile)	Most studies agree that minifundios are too small to be productive. CIDA (1966) studies report that a minifundio can employ less than two people given the income returns, market and technology prevailing and yet we find significant proportions of farms less than two hectares. For example, for Bolivia (1950), 28.7% of the farms are less than 1 hectare, Colombia (1960) 13.7% less than .5 hectares, Chile (1965) 17.8% less than 1 hectare, Ecuador (1954) 26.8% less than 1 hectare, El Salvador (1961) 47.2% less than 1 hectare, Guatemala (1964) 20.4% less than .7 hectares, Peru (1961) 21% less than .5 hectares, Dominican Republic (1960) 44.3% less than 1 hectare. Add that with prices for agricultural products low, and transportation to markets often lengthy and costly, buyers continually exploit minifundio producers in their home region. Also, interest rates for the minifundio owners and landless employee class range from 100-200% in cases where new land purchases are sought. Frequently, credit must be arranged with the latifundista as credit markets are non-existant in rural hinterlands.
Surplus Labor Conditions Persist among the Landless Employee Class, Tenure Rights are Unstable and Non-Agricultural Employment Possibilities are Generally Limited	CIDA (1966), J.D. Coffey (1967; Peruvian Sierra), S.L. Barraclough et.al. (1966), M. Gollas (1970; Guatemala), S.L. Barraclough (1970)	Although data on surplus or redundant labor are scant, the CIDA (1966) studies report than in general 20-30% of the labor supply in rural-agricultural sectors is underemployed in the sense that with increasing organization the same quantity could be produced using existing technology and capital but less labor. In a study of 348 farms less than 2 1/2 hectares in 7 departmentos in Guatemala, it was found that the average farmer spends only 2.8 months of the year working his farm and an average of 3 months as a migrant worker, or 5.8 months in total working per year. In an independent study in rural-agricultural Chile, it was found that 28% of the labor force was in a state of disguised unemployment. Also, a number of studies report latifundio monopsony with respect to purchases of land held intentionally idle to prevent workers from having alternative sources of employment. Given the nature of contracts, the stifling of labor utilization via capital intensive vs. labor intensive technology, extensive farming on latifundios and withholding of land from productivity etc., the landless working class appears to be in a very unstable position. Census of Agriculture figures indicate that the share of rural-agricultural nuclear families that may be subjected to these conditions are for Argentina (1960) 35%, for Brazil (1950) 60%, for Chile (1955) 48%, for Ecuador (1960) 35%. Problems of transportation and proximity add to limited non-farm employment opportunities.

Latifundistas Typically Operate Their Farms Back from Profit Maximizing Points on Their Production Possibility Curves	A.O. Hirschman (1961), M.J. Sternberg (1962; Chile), CEPAL-FAO (1953; Chile), T. Carrol et.al. (1961; Chile), D. Winkleman et.al. (1971;Mexico), P. Moreina (1963; Guatemala), CIDA (1966), D.W. Adams (1967), R.H. Brannon (1969; Uruguay)	Most studies point out that land is owned as an inflationary hedge, as a tax write-off, or for prestige or power reasons. In all cases, accounts of large proportions of either cultivated or irrigated land lying idle are given. In Chile, for example, it was found that 50% of irrigated land on 401 farms was lying idle and in a later study found that out of 479,000 hectares, 44% of the land in natural pastures was lying idle. In Peru (1961), census data reveal that approximately 68% of the land on farms less than five hectares is used for permanent or temporary cultivation as against only 7.5% of the land on farms exceeding 5 hectares. In Chile (1955), farms smaller than 5 hectares averaged approximately 11.5% of their land in natural pastures or wooded areas as against 70% for farms exceeding 5 hectares. In Costa Rica (1955), 79% of the land on minifundios is used for cultivation as against only 12% on latifundios. Whereas Costa Rican minifundios have approximately 18% of their land in pastures or wooded areas, latifundios have approximately 6% of the cultivable land lying idle.
Land is Seldom Farmed Intensively on Latifundios	FAO-IBRD (1959; Peru), J.O. Bray (1966; Chile), CIDA (1966), S.L. Barraclough et.al. (1966), D.F. Fienup et.al. (1969; Argentina), P.R. Crosson (1970; Chile), W.R. Cline (1970; Brazil), A. T. Coutu et.al. (1969; Peru), D. Winkleman et.al. (1971; Mexico), R.A. Berry (1973; Colombia)	Generally, these studies find that land is farmed much more intensively on minifundios than latifundios. In the CIDA (1966) studies, it was found that whereas latifundios occupy 23 times as much land as minifundios, the amount of cultivated land was only 6.5 times as much. Although quality of land was inferior on minifundios, CIDA reports the average value of production per agricultural hectare on minifundios as a multiple of that on latifundios to be for Argentina (1960) 8, Brazil (1960) 5, Chile (1955) 8, Colombia (1960) 14, Ecuador (1954) 3, Guatemala (1950) 4. A general conclusion of these studies is that latifundio land is farmed extensively with capital as against labor intensive production. This is reasoned to be an "efficient" way of avoiding having to supervise peasant workers.

Claim	References	Findings
Large Proportions of Latifundistas can be Characterized as "Absentee Landlords"	CIDA (1966), D.W. Adams et.al.(1967; Colombia), R.J. Clark (1968; Bolivia), T. L. Smith (1967; Colombia), J.R. Riberio et.al. (1969; Brazil), D.W. Adams (1966)	In most cases, accounts of absentee landlords for latifundios sized larger than 500 hectares average about 50%. In Colombia (1960) for example, two thirds of all land on farms exceeding 2000 hectares was operated by managers, whereas in an area of Brazil (1960), 50% of the landlords were absentee with 84% living in towns outside the agricultural state of their farm holding. In Costa Rica (1955), 66% of the latifundio owners were non-resident with 25% without administrators on their holding while absent.
Latifundistas Typically Exploit Their Resident Employees or Occassional Wage Labor	O. Delgado (1965), D.W. Adams (1966; Colombia), R. Youmans et. al. (1968; Colombia), CIDA (1966; Brazil), R. H. Brannon (1969; Uruguay), W.R. Cline (1970; Brazil), CIDA (1966)	The CIDA (1966) studies on Brazil and Chile addressed this issue and found that agricultural employees were receiving less than one half the legal minimum agricultural wage in seven out of eight Brazilian states and that charges for resident housing in both countries were far above legal limits. Other accounts of exploitation focus on verbal contracts of tenant farming which are often broken without warning by latifundistas, and share fees which are adjusted upward when crops are better than average.
Latifundistas Invest very small Proportions of Their Profits back into Their Farms	M. Mamalakis (1965), CIDA (1966; Chile), W.C. Thiesenhusen (1967; Chile), J. O. Bray (1962), D. F. Fienup et.al. (1969; Argentina), R.H. Brannon (1969; Uruguay)	Most researchers agree that latifundistas plough a very small proportion of profits back into their holdings. Claims such as high luxury consumption and investments in other countries are made. On the other hand, non-investment is partially interpreted as "economically rational" behavior given low profit margins, discriminatory agricultural pricing policies (eg., national anti-inflation policies directed at freezing food prices), and the low short-run elasticities of demand for individual products which results in total farm income being often lower for a good than a poor crop yield.

number of assumptions which are fundamental to the development of the model. (Recall that this discussion is limited to those economies with high rates of natural increase, a large proportion of the rural-agricultural population dependent on minifundios, and large proportions of the land being held by latifundistas.)

Assumption 1: The distribution of agricultural land resources to rural-agricultural labor resources is both unequal and relatively fixed in Latin America.

This assumption does not imply, however, that new farms (minifundios, medium-sized farms, and latifundios) have not been established. Admittedly, new land settlements have been undertaken, farms have been subdivided through inheritance rights, and agrarian reforms have made some progress in the redistribution of land (E. Feder 1964). The point here is that in the face of high rates of population growth, slight changes in the structure of land distribution have not resulted in appreciable shifts in the structure of the labor-to-land distribution. Also, rural out-migration has been only partially successful in dampening inequalities in the distribution of agricultural land and incomes or raising income levels.

Assumption 2: A number of forces operate to keep land, capital, technology, and the quality of labor inputs on minifundios relatively constant.

Not only do institutional rigidities prevent free transfer of land resources, but cost of land is typically beyond the means of the minifundio owners or landless workers (CIDA 1966). Rural credit for new farming inputs and marketing facilities for output are typically poorly organized or are organized oligopolistically by latifundistas. This has resulted in (1) high rates of interest for minifundio or landless employee/tenant families, (2) imperfect markets with respect to prices for minifundio or tenant farming output (i.e., markets operated regionally by latifundistas who in turn channel their output to more distant centralized markets offering higher prices), and (3) subsequent impediments to expanding either small farm operations via new land purchases, or output via the addition of costly capital inputs such as new tools and fertilizers. Also, as possibilities for crop rotation on extremely small plots of land are limited and as inputs for improving land quality are costly, land quality is also relatively constant, if not declining.

Assumption 3: Fluctuations in market prices for a range of

agricultural goods are much less important to the subsistence production farm family than to the latifundio in terms of crops chosen
for planting.

The reasoning here is that meeting subsistence needs with respect
to a very narrow range of agricultural products will be the minifundio operator's primary objective. That is, given substantial seasonal
and year-to-year fluctuations in market availability of food crops
and in market prices in most Latin American economies, farmers
fear that if they produce the highest-priced crops for sale and then
buy subsistence crops on the market, they may be caught purchasing
at a time of seasonally or cyclically high prices or low supply (J. W.
Mellor 1969). This means that in the face of price uncertainty they
will tend to farm produce for subsistence needs. The importance of
this assumption lies mainly in its simplifying nature: it allows discussion of minifundio production and accompanying income
possibilities in terms of a rather standard range of products and
market prices. At the same time, however, if market prices of primary subsistence goods increase, there is likely to be an improvement in the minifundio family's income position depending, of
course, on the functioning of the market.

Assumption 4: Neither land nor labor is being used *economically
efficiently* on a large proportion of the latifundios in the sense that
the ratios of *marginal valuation of product of land* (MP_T) to the unit
cost of land (r) are not being equated with the *marginal valuation of
product of labor* (MP_L) to the *unit cost of labor* (w). Rather, $MP_L/w >
MP_T/r$, where T = land, L = labor, w = wage, and r = rent.

This assumption does not imply, however, that the latifundista is
not rational in terms of maximizing his own utilities with respect to
allocating his productive resources. That is, it is the writer's view
that the economic-behavior model when based only on the farm-
firm and profit-maximizing criteria is much too simple to explain
fully the decisions of latifundistas. Rather, the latifundista's entire
occupational structure—especially with respect to his multiple
sources of income—is basic to understanding his maximizing criteria
(E. Feder 1964). For example, idle agricultural land may be merely a
by-product of land purchases as a source of power or prestige, as a
tax write-off, or as a means to fight inflation. Also, there is a likelihood that a backward-bending or at least very inelastic supply curve
on the part of the latifundista for his managerial inputs may be com-
pletely justified in light of possible disutilities associated with having
to (1) supervise hired labor, (2) prepare and manage tenant farm con-

tracts, and/or (3) face possibilities of eventual expropriation of rented land or deterioration of his land under tenant management. This argument would also serve, in part, as a defense for extensive farming and for a capital-intensive as against a labor-intensive production bias. In defense of not intensifying production, it need only be pointed out that given large expanses of relatively productive land, minimal land taxes, and low labor costs under systems of extensive operation, a desired level of income is likely to be readily achieved without intensifying production, increasing productive investment, or adopting modern agricultural technology. Of course, an accompanying argument is that increases in agricultural prices may simply result in a windfall gain accompanied by neither increases in productive investment nor increased agricultural production (R. H. Brannon 1969).

Assumption 5: Tenant farming arrangements are not likely to expand minifundio or landless working family income possibilities much beyond subsistence levels.

The main problem lies in the insecurity of tenure arrangements and uncertainty with regard to income. As noted in Table 2.2, contracts are frequently verbal or, if written, are held by the latifundista only, and may be broken without warning. Traditionally, the concession of land to tenant farmers has been a cheap and convenient way for latifundistas to prepare their land for farming, to start plantations, or to keep the land under crops or livestock. It also attaches the worker to the latifundio—a form of economic and political control—and guarantees the latifundista a plentiful supply of "cheap labor" to meet seasonal requirements. Also, indirect measures are taken to keep investment and improvements on the behalf of the tenant farmer at a minimum, including the following:

1. Workers may be forbidden to plant permanent crops or make improvements on the plots assigned to them;

2. Workers may be kept from planting crops which would earn relatively high cash returns in well-organized markets if the employer also grows them (except in cases of sharecropping);

3. Resident or other workers with the right to use land may be prevented from harvesting their crops, for instance by the employer's insistence that their plots be turned over to pasture for his livestock;

4. Stock-breeding may be restricted to small animals, or all increases may have to be handed over to the landlord in exchange for his permission to breed stock;

5. Workers may be charged heavy fees for minor services (for example, a quarter of the yuca meal ground in the landlord's mill), or high rents for housing;

6. Workers may have to pay large fines for any losses in crops or livestock under their care, whether or not they are responsible.

The final assumptions pertain to the choice behavior of the rural-agricultural labor force participant (and his dependents) with respect to potential migration:

Assumption 6: Labor-force participants are "want satisfiers," and differential perception and assimilation of information pertaining to migration as a means of altering or improving one's state S at place i are not likely to occur unless dissatisfaction with S_i exists.

Migration is interpreted here as a vehicle for *minimizing* physical, social, and economic disutility. Potential migrants are not viewed as persistent calculators of the costs and benefits attached to relocating or remaining inert. Rather, it is assumed that man is a "want satisfier" and that differential perception and assimilation of information pertaining to migration as a means of altering or improving one's state S at place i are not likely to occur unless dissatisfaction with S_i exists. By "dissatisfaction" I mean emergence of noxious events at place i (e.g., absolute or relative deterioration of a neighborhood, or loss of job), or ingrained ambitions and aspirations which cannot be fulfilled at place i (e.g., the inability of educated youngsters to put their skills to work in traditional rural-agricultural settings). An important implication of this assumption is that unless *motivation* to migrate exists, serious decisions about whether or not to migrate are not likely to occur.[5] Evidence and further discussion in support of this position are provided in R. P. Shaw (1974b). An additional implication of this assumption is that (1) previous migration from and return migration to the rural area in question, (2) information flows concerning differential opportunities at alternative places of residence, (3) the existence of friends and relatives in the home or in alternative regions, and (4) the level of education in the potential "sending area," are likely to operate foremost as "conditioners" of the potential migrant's perception of and response to differential economic opportunities.

5. Another way of stating this is that there is no reason to suspect gross inefficiency on behalf of the human mind by assuming that it stores, evaluates, and decides on all place j information vis-a-vis a migration decision, regardless of any interest in the outcome. Insufficient attention to this proposition is the reason for the inadequacy of the cost-return model of migration.

Assumption 7: Labor-force participants will be motivated primarily on economic grounds to migrate to places offering greater economic opportunity if they are confronted with an inability to meet subsistence requirements, i.e., if the marginal valuation of their labor is at or near zero.[6]

Whereas Assumption 6 states that dissatisfaction with S_i is a prerequisite to motivation to migrate, Assumption 7 states that economic considerations will most likely constitute that dissatisfaction if problems of meeting subsistence requirements arise. Now, in the context of a less-developed country (LDC), problems of meeting subsistence requirements are likely to be much greater than in the context of a developed country (DC). Acknowledging differentials in DC versus LDC incomes, income maintenance programs, distribution of incomes, unionization of labor, and governmental social security programs, this point hardly requires elaboration. The economic motive is also likely to be more prevalent in LDCs, given fewer instances of job transfers, and less military, college, health, and retirement migration. In each case, representation in these subgroups in migration flows will be much larger in DC contexts. Overall, empirical studies indicate that economic or work-related reasons for migrating underlie approximately 50 percent of all moves in DCs as against 75-90 percent of all moves in LDCs (R. P. Shaw 1974a). Of course, as the largest proportion of any population is likely to be dependent on family household heads in the labor force, dissatisfaction with an economic state will be represented in migration statistics as the sum of all members of families of the family heads affected.

Now, the assumptions pertaining to land and labor use and the empirical evidence summarized in Table 2.2 imply that income-producing possibilities for a large proportion of Latin America's rural-agricultural labor force are rather dismal. To illustrate how the organization of productive activity in combination with high rates of population increase are likely to create conditions of economic stress and subsequently migration to areas of seemingly greater opportunity, let us now turn to a model relating production possibilities (and therefore farm-family income possibilities) to possibilities for "satisfactory" labor-force participation as family-farm or wage labor.[7] First, we will consider production possibilities and likely

6. A place of greater "economic opportunity" is defined as one offering the individual a greater likelihood of meeting living-level requirements given the differential returns to his labor (labor quality being the same).

7. A situation of "economic stress" will arise when the consumption or living-level requirements of a rural-agricultural family exceed the income-producing

situations of economic stress on minifundios under varying assumptions. Second, we will consider the limited possibilities of extraneous work for minifundio family labor and the landless working class as a means of sustaining living-level requirements. In this case, employment opportunities lie largely in hired farm labor or tenant farming arrangements, and it is argued that the possibilities of either of these opportunities are likely to be severely limited given the nature of productive activity (and subsequently labor demands) on latifundios. Throughout the discussion, it should become apparent how frequently cited migration "pushes" such as low farm incomes, low wages, and unemployment evolve.

CASE I: SITUATIONS OF ECONOMIC STRESS
AND PRODUCTION POSSIBILITIES ON MINIFUNDIOS

While the majority of farms in Latin American agriculture are family owned and operated, a large proportion can be described as subsistence-production family farms (i.e., barely meeting living-level requirements by income in kind or by selling a small proportion of output). Given that returns to on-farm family labor are of primary importance in meeting minifundio household living-level requirements, a necessary departure in an analysis of likely situations of economic stress is to describe the operator's utility profile with respect to his most abundant resource, namely, labor and labor's return.[8]

In the notions of C. Nakajima (1969), the operator's utility function can be expressed as:

(Eq. 1) $U = U(L, Y)$,

subject to the restrictions:

(Eq. 1.1) $\overline{L} \gtreqqless L \gtreqqless 0$

(Eq. 1.2) $Y \gtreqqless Y_0 > 0$

(Eq. 1.3) $U_L < K$

(Eq. 1.4) $U_Y > 0$,

where L = labor, Y = income to labor, U = utility, $\overline{L}$ = some physiological maximum of labor input per year, Y_0 = family sub-

possibilities of the family given its total productive resources (in the notions of R. A. Easterlin 1971).

8. The description of the minifundio operator's utility function can be applied equally well to the latifundista. However, if a latifundista is an absentee landlord, labor input is more likely to correspond to temporary supervision of the farm (i.e., labor effort). Accordingly, the total operating profits from the farm can be considered as the return to his sum efforts in supervising or working the farm while either a resident or nonresident operator.

sistence income requirement, U_L = marginal utility of labor expenditure, K = some value slightly above zero, and U_Y = marginal utility of income.

Graphically, Figure 2.1 conveys that movement from point Z to Z' (i.e., an increase in labor input L_1 to L_2 on line $0L$) decreases total utility unless there is also an increase in income Y (i.e., from Y_1 to Y_2). The slope of the indifference curves $U_1 \ldots U_n$, then, is $-U_L/U_Y (>0)$ and represents the "marginal valuation of family labor."[9] In other terms, $(\partial U/\partial L)/(\partial U/\partial Y) = \partial Y/\partial L$. Which indifference curve $(U_1 \ldots U_n)$ the family head/farm operator is on at time t depends on both the farm's production possibility curve (with respect to Y) and the family's asset position.

Now, assume that (1) only the family head/farm operator is working on the minifundio, (2) the operator's number of dependents is relatively small (e.g., three as against six), (3) living-level requirements (or subsistence requirements) are being met, (4) the family's asset position is zero (as against a likely negative value), (5) Assumption 2—constant land and technology—is in effect, and (6) the average price for output is relatively constant. These assumptions lead to a point of subjective equilibrium with respect to farm-family labor input and serve as the basis for an analysis of likely situations of economic stress on the minifundio.

When the family farm is in equilibrium (as depicted in Figure 2.2), the marginal productivity of labor (curve MP_L in Figure 2.2b) equals the marginal valuation of labor (curve MV_L in Figure 2.2b) and the equilibrium values of labor and income are obtained from

(Eq. 2) $Y = P_X Q(L, H) + A$

(Eq. 2.1) $P_X Q(L, H) = -U_L/U_Y,$

where Q = units of output, P_X = average price per unit of Q, L = labor, H = hectares of land, and A = assets = 0. In other terms, when $A = 0$, $P_X Q = Y = -U_L/U_Y$ and the marginal valuation of labor equals income.

In Figure 2.2a, any point on the curve FY_1 represents a set of labor and income which the family head/farm operator can choose—thus it can be called a family income curve. Only when an indifference curve or utility profile $U_1 \ldots U_n$ touches FY_1 is the family farm in a state of equilibrium E. Accordingly, corresponding to point E on U_2 in Figure 2.2a, the marginal productivity of labor curve MP_L inter-

---

9. "Family labor" in this case refers only to the family head/farm operator. When additional family members are added to the family's labor force, the slope of the indifference curves will represent an aggregate of the family's utility profile with respect to family labor input and family income returns.

sects the marginal valuation of labor curve MV_L at R in Figure 2.2b, thereby establishing L_1 as the equilibrium labor input. Also, in Figure 2.2a, the intersection of the family income curve FY_1 at point K on the subsistence line Y_0Y_0' indicates that at any point below K' on the labor input line $0L$, the marginal valuation of labor will be zero.

It is now instructive to consider the likely effects of (1) changes in the number of dependents in the minifundio household, (2) changes in minifundio land quality, and (3) changes in the minifundio family's asset position, while assuming relatively constant land, technology, capital inputs, and quality of labor in the minifundio's production function. In each case, situations which are likely to create conditions of economic stress are considered. Also, assume for the present that only family-farm work is available. Later, possibilities of tenant farming or wage and salaried labor as a means of supplementing family income will also be considered.

On the minifundio or subsistence-production family farm three conditions tend to create situations of economic stress. These are:

1. With improvements in government-sponsored health and sanitary facilities, declining mortality (especially infant and childhood mortality) and, to a limited extent, increasing fertility add to the operator/household head's number of noneconomically active dependents; consequently his family subsistence requirements increase and his capacity to save and invest or accumulate assets is reduced.

2. Over the long run, in the face of relatively constant capital inputs and size of farm holdings, intensive farming is likely to be accompanied by declining quality of soil, which will tend to reduce the marginal product of labor on the land.

3. A low, zero, or possibly negative family asset position in combination with possible crop failures is likely to lead to situations of indebtedness as well as to insecurity with respect to maintaining living-level requirements in the future.

The effects of conditions 1 and 3 are most likely to be felt immediately and severely, whereas condition 2 is likely to be felt gradually. Of course, interaction of these conditions is likely to intensify economic stress; in turn, their combined effect is likely to be reinforced by factors such as the inability to obtain credit. Tight credit would certainly accentuate condition 2 as well as the impact of condition 3 on meeting subsistence requirements. This would be particularly so if a bad harvest were experienced.

Cases a, b, and c of Figure 2.3 illustrate the ramifications of conditions 1 through 3 on family-farm living-level requirements and in-

Figure 2.1

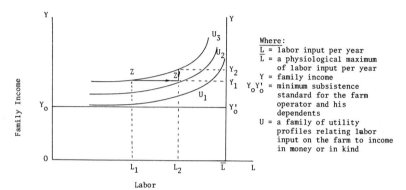

Where:
L = labor input per year
L̄ = a physiological maximum
    of labor input per year
Y = family income
Y₀Y'₀ = minimum subsistence
    standard for the farm
    operator and his
    dependents
U = a family of utility
    profiles relating labor
    input on the farm to income
    in money or in kind

Figure 2.2

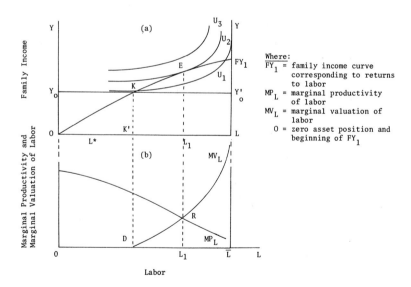

Where:
FY₁ = family income curve
    corresponding to returns
    to labor
MP_L = marginal productivity
    of labor
MV_L = marginal valuation of
    labor
0 = zero asset position and
    beginning of FY₁

Figure 2.3

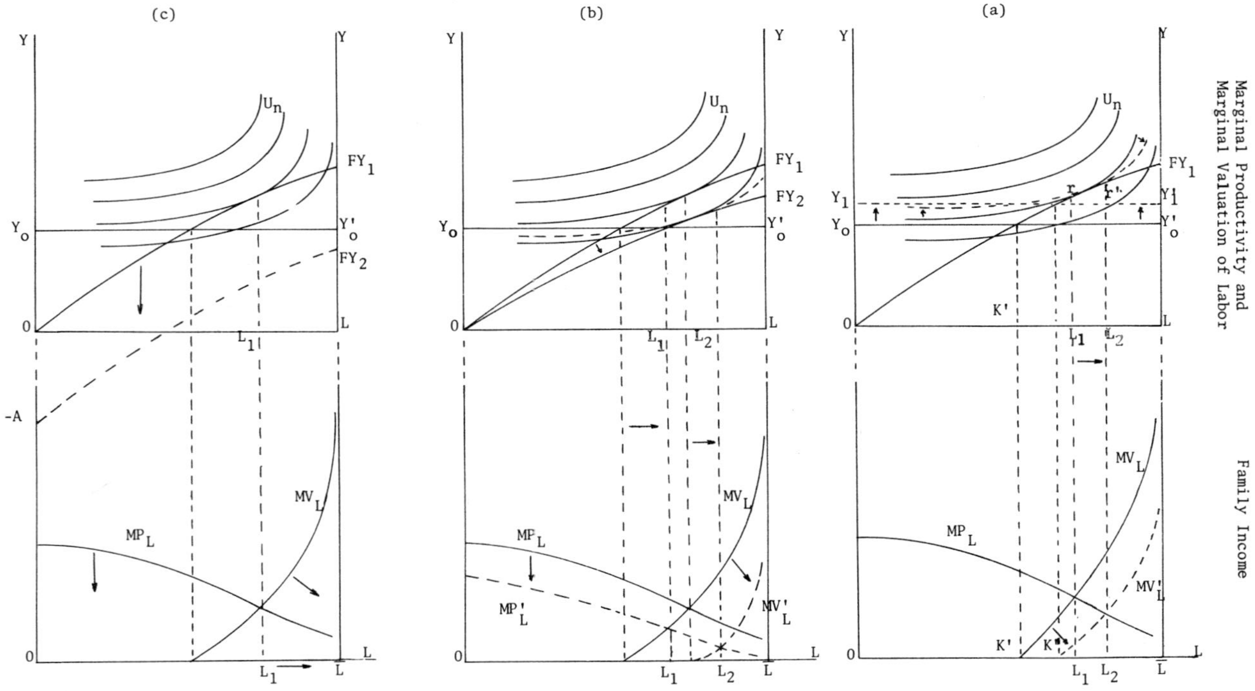

Marginal Productivity and
Marginal Valuation of Labor

Family Income

come-producing possibilities. If condition 1 holds, this will effect a rise in the family subsistence standard line Y_0Y_0' to Y_1Y_1' as shown in Figure 2.3, case a, to the point where the family head/farm operator is working closer to his maximum physiological potential (from L_1 units of labor to L_2 units on line $0L$) merely to meet subsistence demands. This shift in the slope of indifference curve $-U_L/U_Y$ is made since it is likely that the greater the proportion of the operator's labor at which the marginal valuation is below zero, the more he will be inclined to work for a lower rate of return. That is, the shift in the utility profile is indicated in case I(a) by a shift in the point of tangency with the FY_1 curve from r to r'; the increase in the proportion of the operator's labor with the marginal valuation below zero is indicated in the movement of the origin of the MVL curve from point $0K'$ to $0K''$. Condition 2, holding family subsistence requirements constant at Y_0Y_0', brings about the same effect by lowering the marginal product curve MP_L to MP_L' as in case b of Figure 2.3. In turn, this causes not only a drop in the farm-family income curve from FY_1 to FY_2 but a similar shift in the utility profile, a new point of tangency between the family income curve FY_2 and the "new" utility profile (i.e., from point r to r'), and a subsequent increase in the operator's labor input (from L_1 to L_2 on $0L$ corresponding to the new point of subjective equilibrium). Condition 3, case c of Figure 2.3, could plunge the family income curve FY_1 below Y_0Y_0' (the subsistence-living requirement). That is, with a drastic fall in the marginal product to labor curve and a sharp drop in on-farm income possibilities, inability to meet subsistence requirements would probably necessitate either a drain on what assets exist or borrowing. Presuming that borrowing is necessary, the FY curve for the production period $t + 1$ would start below zero at $-A$ and would be likely to contribute to conditions of economic stress in the next period even if climatic conditions, etc., are favorable. Clearly, possibilities for extraneous work would be critical here if living-level requirements were to be maintained.

On the other hand, family labor inputs could be increased, if the assumption of the family head as the only farm labor input is relaxed. In fact, if employment opportunities extraneous to the family farm are limited (we will continue to assume they are nonexistent), family dependents arriving at "economically active ages" will have no alternative but to offer their labor for family-farm production.[10] It is important to ask, then, "In the event that employ-

10. The rate at which family dependents arrive at "economically active ages" is

ment opportunities extraneous to the family farm are not available, is the addition of labor to the family farm likely to increase output enough to meet family subsistence requirements?"[11] On the basis of CIDA (1966) estimates that a minifundio can employ less than two people, given the income returns, market, and technology prevailing in Latin American agriculture, and that an average of 30-50 percent of the farms are less than 1 hectare in size, the answer is likely to be "no." Figure 2.4 relates the impact of one, two, then three workers on the minifundio family income curve with the indifference curves representing the family's aggregate utility profile. The subsistence requirement line $Y_0 Y_0'$ is shown to increase fractionally to $Y_1 Y_1'$ and then to $Y_2 Y_2'$ as workers are added, given likely increases in food consumption requirements as family members shift to worker status. In this case, the number of dependents, the land quality, and climatic conditions are assumed constant.

As the number of workers increases from one to three, the physiological labor input maximum increases from $1\bar{L}$ to $3\bar{L}$. However, with all other factor inputs held constant, the MP_L curve will eventually approach zero as labor inputs are increased. If this implies that at some point increasing labor input is accompanied by an extremely low return to labor or no return at all (i.e., the FY curve flattens out), the proportion of unused or surplus labor on the farm can be expected to increase, from $1\bar{L} - \bar{L}_1$ to $3\bar{L} - L_3$. Also, if employment opportunities extraneous to the family farm are not available, it is likely that as the proportion of unused family labor increases, a situation of economic stress will evolve.

Thus far focus has been on an important segment of Latin America's rural-agricultural labor force and what would appear to be its most immediate source of income-producing possibilities. Given high rates of natural increase, increasing dependency ratios, and, over time, continual additions to the farm-family work force, there is little doubt that additional means of income-producing ac-

---

also a consideration. For example, labor-force accession rates could be constant and unchanging if fertility and mortality rates had been relatively constant over the last few decades. In the case of Latin America, however, most economies are experiencing declining mortality (particularly infant and child mortality) and relatively constant, if not increasing, fertility rates. This has resulted in higher rates of labor-force accession (lagged accordingly).

11. The possibility of little available work extraneous to the farm is very real in many rural provincial regions of Latin American countries such as Chile and Peru, where farms larger than 2,500 hectares exist in close proximity to minifundios but employ very little wage or tenant labor.

Figure 2.4

Marginal Productivity and   Family Income
Marginal Valuation of Labor

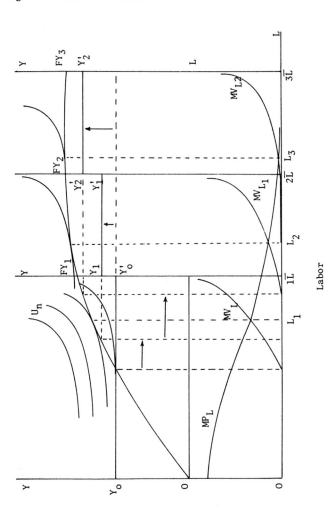

tivity are of critical importance to the minifundio farm family. Let us now relax the assumption that employment opportunities extraneous to the minifundio farm family are nonexistent.

The most immediate alternative income-producing possibilities (in terms of proximity) are likely to lie in either farming someone else's land (on a sharecropping or fixed-rent basis) or joining the wage- and salary-earning agricultural labor force. In either case, the worker will be entering a competitive and in many cases exploitative labor market. It is the author's position that income-producing possibilities in either of these cases are likely to be severely limited given the nature of productive activity (and the subsequent labor demand) by those owning large tracts of land. Accordingly, it is of some importance to discuss production possibilities on the latifundio.

CASE II: PRODUCTION POSSIBILITIES
AND LABOR DEMANDS ON LATIFUNDIOS

Productive activity on latifundios can be differentiated from that on minifundios on the following grounds:

1. The majority of latifundios are commercial farms producing goods largely for sale;

2. The latifundista is likely to be responsive to price changes and to operate as a price taker;[12]

3. Technological change characterizes the latifundio's production function and land is likely to be farmed extensively;

4. Land is not fixed and usually productive activity can be expanded within the latifundio's own resource boundaries.

Unlike the discussion of income-producing possibilities on the minifundio, interest in the latifundio is more with factors tending to impede or stimulate absorption of rural-agricultural labor as either wage, salary, or contract labor. Accordingly, the behavior of latifundistas with respect to utilization of labor as against alternative factor inputs will have considerable bearing on the capacity of local rural labor markets to contend with the available supply of labor.

Factors likely to play a significant role in conditioning the "behavior" of the latifundista with respect to utilization of labor inputs on his family farm include (1) his asset position; (2) his

12. Although we have characterized the latifundista as a "monopolist" in terms of his ability to influence (1) the price of land, (2) credit interest rates, and (3) regional labor demand, we do not expect him to be able to operate as a "price maker" with respect to the sale of his farm output.

preferences for capital-intensive technology and extensive land-use for prestige reasons, as a means to avoid having to supervise labor, etc.; (3) the degree of price uncertainty or difficulties in market distribution of output; and (4) whether his land has been purchased for power or prestige reasons, as a tax write-off, or as an inflationary hedge.

To illustrate how these factors may operate to curtail rural-agricultural labor demand (and therefore employment), consider again the family of indifference curves $U_0 \ldots U_n$, and a latifundio family income curve as in Figure 2.5.[13] In part a, the curve FY_1 represents net farm income returns to the latifundista with $0L$ representing either the latifundista's personal effort in supervising the farming operation or the farm's total wage, salary, and tenant farm labor input.

The first point to consider is that if there is a tendency not to operate the latifundio at its profit-maximizing point on its production possibility curve (Assumption 4), then the higher the latifundio's asset position (i.e., raising FY_1 to FY_2 with a positive asset position A in Figure 2.5a), the less will be its labor input (either personal or total labor inputs), and therefore the less aggregate labor will be demanded (i.e., the shift in labor input from L_2 to L_1 in Figure 2.5b). This point accords with the view that the latifundista's typically high asset position facilitates absenteeism and purchase of land for power, each of which is likely to be associated with unutilized land.

To illustrate the impact of preferences for capital-intensive technology (e.g., for prestige reasons) or capital-extensive farming (to avoid surveillance of hired and tenant labor) on the amount of labor demanded, consider Figure 2.6. Part b relates a number of alternate factor input combinations available to the latifundista. These can be viewed as technological combinations shown as A, B, or C in Figure 2.6b. Accordingly, vectors $0a' = 0b' = 0c'$ represent the same quantity of output attainable using either technological combination. Actually, in the underdeveloped economy with an abundant labor supply, wr represents the cheapest factor allocation line in terms of the cost of factor inputs demanded by either technique A, B, or C, whereas $w'r'$ reduces labor input L_2 to L_1 and therefore labor demanded by the latifundio. The position taken here is that the choice of capital-intensive technology is widespread enough so that ag-

13. As noted previously, in this context labor absorption pertains particularly to the sum of all labor offered for wages, salaries, or tenant farming by those of economically active ages on minifundios or in the landless employee class.

Figure 2.5

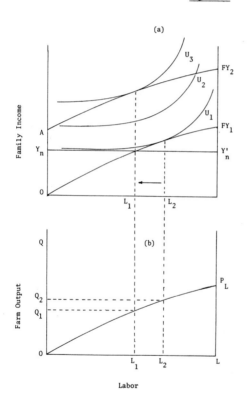

Where:
A = a positive asset
position and the
beginning of FY_2
Q = output
F_L = productivity curve of
labor with a given pro-
duction function
$Y_n Y'_n$ = income requirements
to sustain the latifundista's
style of living

Figure 2.6

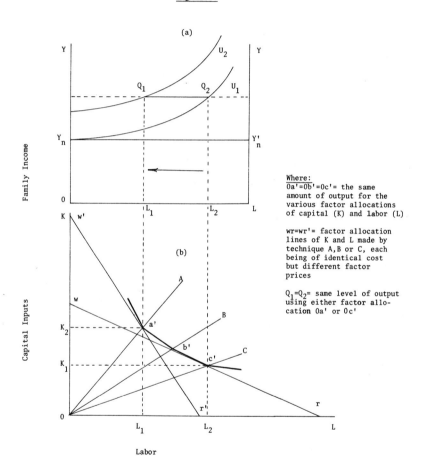

(a)

(b)

Where:
$\overline{0a'}=\overline{0b'}=0c'=$ the same
amount of output for the
various factor allocations
of capital (K) and labor (L)

wr=wr'= factor allocation
lines of K and L made by
technique A,B or C, each
being of identical cost
but different factor
prices

$Q_1=Q_2=$ same level of output
using either factor allo-
cation 0a' or 0c'

Family Income

Capital Inputs

Labor

Figure 2.7

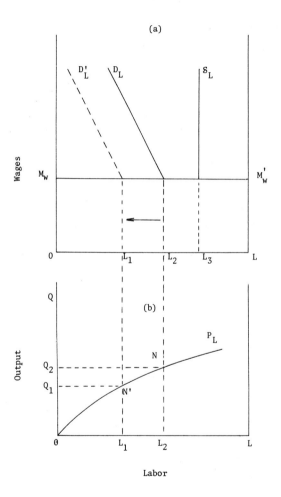

(a)

Wages

D'_L D_L S_L

M_W ————————————————— M'_W

0   L_1 L_2 L_3 L

Where:
$\underline{D_L}$ = demand for labor
S_L = supply of labor
$M_W M'_W$ = minimum legal or
            subsistance wage
P_L = productivity of
        labor curve

(b)

Q

Output

                          P_L
                    N
Q_2 ————————
Q_1 ——————
              N'

0   L_1 L_2 L

Labor

gregately latifundios contribute to the inability of the labor market to contend with a continually growing rural labor supply.[14]

Finally, given recognized imperfections in market distribution of agricultural output in rural Latin America, labor demand is likely to be cut back considerably as market distribution problems arise. This possibility is illustrated in Figure 2.7, where a surplus labor condition $(L_3 - L_2)$ is indicated, labor is abundant at a subsistence wage, and at point N the latifundio is presumed to be operating on a profit-maximizing basis relative to market demand for output. Given difficulties in market distribution of output, however (e.g., the inability to sell output $Q_2 - Q_1$ at market prices or to sell output at all), the latifundio owner is likely to be forced to a "nonoptimum" position on his production possibility curve, thereby decreasing labor inputs (i.e., labor demand) from L_2 to L_1.[15] As this possibility is likely to be particularly sensitive to market inefficiencies in specific regions or to the regional or national economic climate with respect to demands for particular agricultural goods (for example, a decline in demands for exports), the severity of its impact on the rural labor market is likely to fluctuate.

Each of these illustrations conveys that the latifundista's orientation to agricultural productivity is likely to have negative ramifications on the income-earning potentialities and aspirations of wage- and salary-seeking minifundio or landless workers. It would add little to the analysis to further illustrate optimum allocations of minifundio family labor on the family farm in combination with extraneous farm wage or tenant farming opportunities, or the limited role that off-farm employment might play in raising earning capacity. The main point here (i.e., in case II) is that economic stress on the minifundio or among the landless peasantry is not likely to be alleviated by a labor market reliant upon the labor demands of latifundios. Rather, the latifundista's orientation to productive activity is more likely to operate as a barrier only beyond which can evolve

14. To an extent, different factor combinations could also result from differences in factor costs between small units using family labor and large units using hired labor. First, capital costs including interest (or inability to acquire credit due to lack of assets for collateral) will be higher on small farms than on large ones. This will tend to encourage more intensive labor use. Second, the "cost" of labor on smaller family farms will be the opportunity cost which, in the absence of alternative employment opportunities, will be apt to reduce the "cost" of such labor below the going hired-labor wage rate. Third, if public policy tends to hold cost of capital, to those with access to credit, below general market rates, then capital-intensive production on larger farms would be more frequently encountered.

15. That is, "nonoptimum" from the viewpoint of the social economy but "optimum" for the individual given the market he faces.

a more favorable distribution of land to labor resources and increased income-producing possibilities.

OUT-MIGRATION AS AN ALTERNATIVE

An implication of the assumptions and the development of the model in cases I and II is that in rural Latin America, certain population subgroups (and within those subgroups particular members) are more likely to experience economic stress than others. Specifically, members of minifundio farm families and landless working families are expected to demonstrate the highest propensity to migrate to areas offering seemingly great opportunity.

Whether the decision to migrate is as an act of sheer desperation as suggested in one Chilean study (W. C. Thiesenhusen 1966), or is based largely on perceived positive urban employment and income differentials (and in some cases opportunities in alternative rural-farming areas), is an important question. The hypothesis advanced here (in keeping with Assumption 6) is that motivation to migrate will be initiated by the emergence of noxious or unsatisfactory conditions in the rural sector. Once migration is considered, information on rural-urban income and amenity differentials is expected to be actively sought as part of the decision whether or not to actually migrate. In other terms, rural "pushes" may operate both directly and indirectly in creating motivation to migrate, whereas urban "pulls" may operate largely as "conditioners" of decisions on where to migrate. If so, this would help explain why rural-urban migration flows persist in the face of high rates of urban unemployment, serious urban housing shortages, and insignificant amenity differentials (therefore adding to these problems). The chapter to follow seeks to test some of these relations.

3. Statistical Model

THOROUGH TESTING of the theoretical model requires much more extensive data than are currently available from census or survey sources. One problem involves the disaggregation of estimates of rural out-migration. Although magnitudes of rural out-migrants of labor-force ages can be estimated, it is not possible to discern whether the migrants are (1) minifundio family heads (with or without dependents), (2) landless family heads (with or without dependents), (3) members of tenant or sharecropper families, (4) members of latifundio families, (5) those just arriving at economically active ages on minifundios or in the landless worker class, or (6) those who are migrating for purposes of schooling, retirement, or the military. Accordingly, it will not be possible to differentiate the migration behavior of these specific population subgroups relative to the variety of factors purported in the previous chapter to be the prime determinants of situations of economic stress. As for testing for the presence of determinants of situations of economic stress including availability of credit, asset positions, and employment opportunities for first-job seekers, data are equally scarce.

On the other hand, it is possible to devise estimates of rural out-migration for which the population "at risk" is largely dependent on agriculture as minifundio workers or as landless agricultural employees. It is also possible to devise measures of the interaction of population growth effects with aspects of the structure of the land-tenure system in the rural "sending areas" and to hypothesize their expected influence on migration behavior in accordance with the theoretical model. Using aggregative statistical techniques, a number of additional factors likely to influence migration can be examined simultaneously, thereby providing a means of evaluating the relative importance of the "agricultural factor" in accounting for variations in migration behavior. This is the procedure adopted in evaluating the potential of the theoretical model for understanding migration behavior in rural Chile, Peru, Costa Rica, and Colombia.

The burden of the empirical analysis relies on cross-sectional data at the provincial level in four Latin American countries, Chile (1952-60), Peru (1940-61), Colombia (1951-64), and Costa Rica (1950-63). Although rural-urban migration flows demonstrate unique characteristics in each country, the interaction of population growth effects and the structure of land tenure will be assumed to be the dominant influence in provincial net rural migration in Chile and Peru, less so in Colombia, and much less so in Costa Rica.

As an illustration of inequalities in the provincial distribution of land to labor and population growth in each country, consider Table 3.1. In Chile and Peru, and to a lesser extent in Colombia, the distribution of labor to land is extremely uneven; population growth rates are typically high, and the system of land tenure has been described extensively in qualitative studies as inhibiting income-producing possibilities for the majority of the rural-agricultural labor force. As a contrast, the distribution of labor to land resources is much less uneven in Costa Rica, although, again, population growth rates are very high.

Of course, as is evident in Table 3.1, within each country there are significant variations in the population growth rates and characteristics of the land-tenure system. Accordingly both within- and between-country analyses should provide a good indication of the extent to which the interaction of population growth with the system of land tenure and, consequently, income-producing possibilities within the minifundio-latifundio complex influence migration.

In the analysis of the determinants of provincial rural out-migration in Chile and Peru, use is made of a multiple-regression model. The migration experience of each country is examined separately. For Costa Rica and Colombia, a graphic analysis is presented, as the small number of provinces and lack of data for Colombia inhibit the effectiveness of the regression technique. As the quantitative

Table 3.1. Structure of Land Tenure and Population Growth Rates by Province for Chile (1952-60),
Peru (1940-61), Costa Rica (1950-63), and Colombia (1951-64)

Province	Minifundios[a]			Latifundios[a]			Annual Provincial Rates of Natural Increase
	% Farms	% Provincial Land	Average Size in Hectares	% Farms	% Provincial Land	Average Size in Hectares	
Chile							
Aconcagua	64.6	0.4	1.5	2.3	94.9	9,573	2.87
Valparaíso	70.1	0.8	0.8	3.0	74.3	1,672	2.55
O'Higgins	71.8	1.6	1.1	1.9	73.6	1,867	2.97
Colchagua	67.1	0.6	1.1	3.6	79.6	1,538	2.91
Curicó	41.3	0.4	1.2	4.2	73.2	1,394	2.86
Talca	26.5	0.3	1.9	5.7	76.8	2,233	2.60
Maule	19.4	0.4	1.8	3.6	52.1	1,207	2.38
Linares	42.9	0.6	1.3	3.5	76.6	1,925	2.56
Ñuble	37.0	0.9	1.4	2.9	61.7	1,878	2.40
Bío-Bío	25.9	0.2	1.7	5.2	72.9	2,015	2.55
Malleco	16.3	0.1	0.9	4.9	70.7	2,215	2.41
Cautín	17.9	0.2	0.9	3.4	39.3	1,161	1.60
Osorno	23.4	0.1	0.7	6.9	68.0	1,530	2.28
Llanquihue	17.4	0.2	1.3	3.1	58.7	2,040	2.53
Santiago	56.3	0.4	1.0	3.7	88.0	3,631	2.92
Peru							
Tumbes	92.4	5.6	1.0	0.07	88.0	25,000	3.50
Piura	90.0	6.8	1.1	0.02	82.2	6,471	3.20
Cajamarca	79.9	12.8	1.8	0.18	59.2	3,769	3.03
Lambayeque	76.0	3.5	1.5	0.25	82.6	10,634	3.23

Province	Minifundios[a]			Latifundios[a]			Annual Provincial Rates of Natural Increase
	% Farms	% Provincial Land	Average Size in Hectares	% Farms	% Provincial Land	Average Size in Hectares	
La Libertad	78.4	4.4	1.8	0.30	84.4	7,631	2.76
Ancash	89.3	9.1	1.5	0.30	74.3	3,443	3.07
Huánuco	77.5	4.8	1.8	0.26	63.0	3,637	1.13
Junín	88.8	4.3	1.1	0.30	76.5	6,033	2.13
Lima	84.2	4.4	1.3	0.50	75.3	3,469	2.40
Ica	73.0	9.7	1.2	0.80	49.0	1,352	2.27
Huancavelica	91.1	14.4	1.5	0.20	68.8	3,270	1.37
Ayacucho	88.0	4.3	1.1	0.25	56.3	2,248	1.00
Cuzco	88.0	6.2	1.1	0.70	81.1	3,029	1.40
Apurímac	93.0	3.3	1.1	0.25	82.3	5,035	1.60
Puno	83.6	4.7	1.2	0.90	80.0	2,948	1.40
Moquegua	93.0	5.7	1.1	0.20	90.0	10,814	2.03
Tacna	75.1	10.7	1.3	0.80	70.0	2,598	2.00
Loreto	82.2	5.5	1.2	0.20	66.7	4,426	2.40
San Martín	31.2	2.1	3.2	0.08	9.2	1,427	2.87
Costa Rica							
Alajuela	47.0	14.4	2.7	0.34	17.5	1,160	4.00
Cartago	55.0	9.1	2.6	0.80	35.2	1,442	4.20
Heredia	65.4	17.3	2.5	0.60	28.7	1,106	3.90
Guanacaste	30.9	2.2	3.1	0.86	52.4	4,480	4.65
Puntarenas	24.9	4.0	3.1	0.76	23.7	1,688	4.85
Limón	43.0	5.3	3.4	1.03	52.0	2,331	3.95

Colombia

Antioquia	70.5	5.7	1.3	0.4	28.8	1,065	3.77
Atlántico	66.5	3.8	1.3	0.6	21.0	816	3.36
Bolívar	62.5	3.0	1.4	1.0	37.1	1,102	2.83
Boyacá	68.6	5.6	1.6	0.6	62.0	2,250	2.91
Cauca	63.1	9.1	1.9	0.3	23.3	1,153	2.41
Cundinamarca	69.4	11.2	1.7	0.2	18.5	1,013	3.40
Huila	47.0	3.0	1.8	0.7	29.8	1,074	2.99
Magdalena	54.4	1.2	1.3	2.2	49.7	1,352	2.87
Nariño	67.3	16.0	1.8	0.1	8.2	860	2.51
Notre de Santander	38.5	3.9	2.2	0.4	17.7	1,079	3.52
Santander	51.3	5.1	2.0	0.5	24.2	950	2.90
Tolima	51.9	4.0	1.7	0.6	27.3	1,020	2.22

a. A minifundio is defined as a farm holding of less than 5 hectares. In the case of Costa Rica, census classifications require that a minifundio be defined as a farm holding of less than 3.5 hectares or 7 hectares. The latter is used here. Latifundios are generally defined as farm holdings in excess of 500 hectares except in the case of Costa Rica, where a latifundio is defined as a farm holding in excess of 700 hectares. All data are taken from respective national agricultural censuses.

model requires a dependent-variable, independent-variable format (i.e., the property to be "explained" as against the "predictor" or "explanatory variables"), the measure of migration and hypothesized determinants are presented below in this manner.[1] The regression results and graphic analysis will be presented in the following chapter.

DEPENDENT VARIABLE

To measure rural out-migration in each country, rates of total net provincial rural male labor-force migrants per 100 average provincial rural male members of the labor force over the country's census interval have been estimated.[2] For Chile these rates are denoted by the symbol M_C, for Peru, M_P, for Costa Rica, M_{CR}, and for Colombia, M_{COL}. Procedures used in calculating the rates and some problems encountered are summarized in Appendix II. For each within-country analysis, total net provincial rural male labor-force migration rates are used, whereas for between-country analysis, total net migration rates are transformed to yearly net average rates. For the regressions, observations for M_C range from 13.1 to 2.4, and for M_P, from 12.1 to −2.3, thereby insuring a good range of variation in each country.[3]

To insure that the provincial rural male labor-force migrants are taken largely from an agricultural background, only those provinces in which a large majority of the provincial rural economically active males work in agricultural occupations in the agricultural industry have been included in the within-country analysis. Arbitrarily a "large majority" was considered to be 80 percent or more. Including only those provinces in which the rural and agricultural sectors can be largely equated permits a more rigorous test of the in-

---

1. Aggregative statistical models do not actually explain the "behavior" of the dependent variable (that is, movements in its magnitude), but provide a measure of the extent to which movements in the magnitudes of the independent variables are associated with variations in the dependent variable. Any inference about causality must be based on a sound theoretical framework, for which the aggregative statistical model serves best as an empirical test.

2. For each country, measures of independent and dependent variables are represented as one (average) observation per province for the complete time period examined (as distinct from one observation per province per year based on a pooling of time-series and cross-sectional data).

3. In the provincial analyses, a positive rate of migration indicates provincial net out-migration, whereas a negative rate indicates in-migration.

fluence of the system of land tenure on rural migration behavior. Also, exclusion of a number of provinces in each country will not significantly affect the implications of our findings for the country as a whole, as for Chile approximately 84 percent of the country's total rural male labor force and 75 percent of its total rural labor force are represented, for Peru approximately 93 percent of the country's total rural male labor force and 76 percent of its total rural labor force are represented, and for Costa Rica approximately 76 percent of the country's total rural male labor force and 69 percent of its total rural labor force are represented. All Colombian provinces meeting data requirements also met the 80 percent criterion.

For similar reasons the rates of provincial rural out-migration have been calculated for males only (except in the case of Colombia, where required data were not available). First, the rural female labor force in each country is relatively unimportant, accounting for only 13 percent of the total rural labor force in Chile, 18 percent in Peru, 13 percent in Colombia, and 8 percent in Costa Rica. Also, a significant proportion of the rural females economically active in each country is engaged in nonagricultural activities—42 percent in rural Chile, 21 percent in rural Peru, 78 percent in rural Costa Rica, and 40 percent in Colombia. Accordingly, as economically active males are most likely to be both rural-agricultural household heads and the principal income earners, analysis of the migration behavior of this group relative to conditions in the agricultural industry should yield a more rigorous test of our model.[4]

SELECTION OF INDEPENDENT VARIABLES
AND HYPOTHESES

The Structure of Land Tenure and Population Growth Rates.—As the central argument of this inquiry is that the nature of the land-tenure system, in combination with high population growth rates, interacts to create situations of inadequate agricultural opportunity, it is important to devise a measure of these influences and relate it to the

4. This is not to say, however, that rural-urban female migration is insignificant or determined by the same forces as those that influence rural-urban male migration. As noted in Chapter 1, as many females as males migrate from rural to urban areas, if not more. Domestic work in urban areas was also cited as exercising a unique pull on rural females. On the other hand, if a number of institutional factors "condition" the rural labor market to the extent that income-earning possibilities are in short supply for males, these same factors may limit opportunities for females. An indication that

measure of out-migration. Basic to such a measure is the distribution of rural population or labor force to the distribution of available land. That is, by taking into consideration provincial differences in the concentration of the rural population to available arable land, as well as the effect of provincial differences in the proportion of the available arable land held by latifundistas, the stock of demands on the land for both employment and livelihood can be estimated. At the same time, by incorporating the effects of provincial rates of natural increase, the flow of population and labor-force demands on the land can be estimated. In either case the stock and flow estimates serve as indexes of population pressure and agricultural inopportunity.

The principal measures to be used in the regression analysis, then, can be defined as follows:[5]

Stock index of population pressure and agricultural inopportunity:

$$\frac{P_t - f(L_o + L_w + F_o)}{T_A - L_A}$$

Flow index of population pressure and agricultural inopportunity:

$$\frac{\left[P_t(1 + r)^n - P_t\right] - \left[f(L_o + L_w + F_o)(1 + r)^n - f(L_o + L_w + F_o)t\right]}{T_A - L_A}$$

where P_t = provincial rural-agricultural population at time t; f = average rural family size of each province at time t; L_o = latifundio owners in each province; L_w = latifundio full-time employees in each province; F_o = owners of intermediate-sized farms in each

this may be so was found in the regression analysis of provincial rural out-migration in Chile (Chapter 4), where the degree of association between measures of agricultural inopportunity and M_C was largely unaltered when M_C was related not to male migration but to total-population rural-urban migration. Of course, there is also the possibility that a large proportion of females may migrate as dependents of male household heads and that this is reflected in the above results.

5.   The measure of rural emigration is actually a rate-per-unit-of-time flow. This implies that all of the independent variables should also be represented as flows. Furthermore, it would be useful to consider not just rate-per-unit-of-time flows, but changes in these rates. The main obstacle to operationalizing all independent variables as flows is the general lack of data of sufficient quantity and quality.

province (that is, 5 to 500 hectares); r = provincial (rural) rate of natural increase from t to $t + n$; n = years from time t to $t + n$; T_A = total provincial arable agricultural land (that is, total nonsterile land minus natural pasture land and forested land); and L_A = provincial arable agricultural land held by latifundistas.

In the stock index, P_t represents the total rural provincial population dependent on the land at time t. From this population the stock of all workers and their dependents expected not to be confronted by situations of economic stress is estimated, that is, latifundio owners and their dependents, full-time latifundio employees and their dependents, and owner-operators of medium-sized farms and their dependents (see Appendix III for provincial values for each variable and additional notes on the derivation of the measures). The numerator, then, as a population at risk, corresponds roughly with those population subgroups expected to demonstrate the greatest propensity to migrate.[6]

As a gauge of the agricultural opportunities available to the majority of the rural-agricultural labor force, provincial arable land held by latifundistas (L_A) is subtracted from the total provincial arable land (T_A). This step accords with the author's argument that as latifundio land is typically farmed extensively and as large tracts of latifundio land lie idle, exclusion of this land from the total arable land base will yield a closer approximation of the range of agricultural income-producing possibilities. However, as this is not the case in all provinces, the role of the latifundio in either creating employment opportunities for the landless employee class or providing alternative sources of income for minifundio workers is taken into consideration in the numerator of the index (i.e., L_{wf}). As for the arable land available to the majority of the rural population, this includes land both owned and operated by minifundio farm families and intermediate-sized farms. The latter are included as it is expected that owners of intermediate-sized farms operate on or close to the frontiers of their production possibility curves by utilizing more labor-intensive technology than latifundios and employ more substantial proportions of both full- and part-time labor.

6. An alternative approach would be to drop P_t and f and replace P_t with a measure of total labor force at time t. One problem, however, is that a measure of labor force does not incorporate the effects of differentials in the dependent population (and, therefore, total consumption demands "on the land"), which are likely to vary considerably between areas, due to differentials in mortality, fertility, and, therefore, dependency.

In the flow index, $P_t(1 + r)^n$ represents the total rural provincial population dependent on the land at time t "operated upon" by the provincial rates of natural increase in effect from time t to $t + n$. By subtracting P_t from $P_t(1 + r)^n$, the growth in population (i.e., the flow) in the absence of migration is estimated. At the same time, by applying the same provincial "growth operator" to the component $f(L_0 + L_w + F_0)_t$ and by subtracting the result from $f(L_0 + L_w + F_0)_t$, a measure of flow is also estimated for this population subgroup. The same population "growth operator" is used in both flow estimates, as data limitations do not allow derivation of more "group-specific" growth operators. (See Appendix III for exemplary derivations of the stock and flow indexes.)

A minor problem in both indexes concerns the time reference for the denominator $(T_A - L_A)$. In the stock index, the time reference is t (i.e., for Chile $t = 1952$), whereas in the flow index, the time reference is t to $t + n$ (i.e., for Chile, from 1952 to 1960) and growth over the time interval. The time reference for $(T_A - L_A)$, however, lies somewhere between t and $t + n$ (i.e., for Chile, 1955), and in the case of the flow index, it is not possible to estimate growth in $(T_A - L_A)$ over the time interval. Again, data limitations are at the base of the problem as data for the sample countries, and the empirical time referents, are available for only the first national census of agriculture. This problem should be a minor one, however, as the structure of land distribution (the proportion of land available to the majority of the rural population as against that held by latifundistas) is not likely to have changed much over short time intervals.[7] As for land resettlement and redistribution programs, their overall impact has been minor up to the late 1950s for the majority of the economies of Latin America.

> *Hypothesis I—The central proposition to be tested, then, is that as the stock or flow indexes of population pressure and agricultural inopportunity increase, the incidence of rural out-migration will increase. If, in fact, the system of land tenure is playing a major role in "influencing" situations of economic stress and, consequently, rural out-migration behavior, varia-*

7. For example, the big land invasions and the semivoluntary sale of Sierra haciendas to their workers only began in a big way in Peru after 1962, though there were skirmishes earlier. In Chile the peasant movement was broken in 1947 and only recovered and resumed in 1965.

tions in this index should account for the majority of
the variation in our dependent variable.[8]

In studying the relative importance of the stock and flow indexes, the index incorporating the flow alone should be most highly associated with the measure of out-migration. That is, if opportunities are in short supply at time *t*, and rates of population natural increase are on the upswing, then we would expect a greater (or increasing) disequilibrium between the demand and supply of income-earning possibilities (or living-level requirements) during the period *t* to *t* + *n*. On the other hand, if rates of natural increase *r* do not vary substantially between provinces and if the flow is generally proportional to the stock in each province, then both the indexes may be equally correlated with the measure of out-migration. As for the stock index, we would expect a disequilibrium to arise between the demand and supply of living-level requirements due to such factors as the previously mentioned soil erosion of available arable land, increasing monopolization of agricultural resources by latifundistas, and greater discontent with the organization of productive activity due to increased educational and literacy levels.

As an additional means of evaluating the significance of aspects of the structure of land tenure in the migration process, a number of direct measures relating to land and labor distribution are also included. For example, measures of the proportion of provincial farms that are minifundios, the proportion of total agricultural land held by latifundistas, the proportion of the province's labor force on minifundios weighted by population rates of natural increase, and the proportion of the labor force that are agricultural employees are all included in the regressions. Simpler population-to-land-density measures have also been included as a means of checking on the utility of the more elaborate stock and flow indexes (e.g., these measures as against the provincial rural population to total provincial nonsterile agricultural land or total provincial arable land). In each case the hypothesized relationship is positive. In more formal terms, the rationale behind our hypotheses can be stated as follows:

Hypothesis Ia—Given the description of conditions on minifundios, we may expect that *the larger the proportion of the rural population centralized on minifundios,* the

8. The italicized portion represents the relationship that can actually be tested in the empirical analysis.

greater the likelihood of situations of economic stress and *the greater the incidence of rural out-migration. By taking into consideration population growth rates on minifundios, this relationship should increase significantly* given the additional demands on the minifundio household head to provide for his dependents or the improbability of those arriving at economically active ages on minifundios (i.e., a lagged effect) "earning" a satisfactory return on their labor.

Hypothesis Ib—Given the description of the use of land on latifundios and the role of the latifundista in providing employment opportunities for the minifundio and landless employee class, we may expect that *the larger the proportion of the agricultural land held by the latifundistas, the higher the incidence of rural out-migration should be.*

Hypothesis Ic—Given the description of income-producing possibilities confronting the landless employee class, and as this group is not likely to be tied to the rural sector by agricultural investments or farm ownership, we may expect that *the larger this rural population subgroup, the greater the incidence of rural out-migration.*

Hypothesis Id—If, in fact, latifundismo plays a major role in influencing income-earning possibilities on the land, then *measures of population pressure incorporating the effects of latifundismo (that is, our stock and flow indexes) should be much more highly associated with rural out-migration than simpler population-to-land measures which exclude the effects of latifundismo on the availability of arable land.*

Although it might be argued that Hypotheses Ia, Ib, and Ic are really subsumed under Hypothesis I, the main concern is to check the significance and consistency of the relationship between the stock and flow indexes against the findings for the more direct measures of agricultural inopportunity. It is also possible to evaluate the assumption that those dependent on latifundios and inter-mediate-sized farms, shown by $f(L_o + L_w + F_o)$, are less "afflicted" by situations of economic stress and are, therefore, less likely to migrate. That is, by excluding the component $f(L_0 + L_w + F_0)$ from the stock and flow indexes, the assumption will be supported if the resulting correlation coefficient with the measure of out-migration is lower. Should discrepancies exist in any of the above, this will call into question the utility of both the measures and the theoretical model.

Additional Considerations.—In addition to the variables and hy-potheses presented above, it is important to consider other possible determinants of migration for at least three reasons. First, theoretical and empirical studies in both Latin American and other contexts point to the significance of a number of influences in migration behavior such as (1) urban-rural wage and employment differentials, (2) education and literacy, (3) availability of transportation, (4) prox-imity of urban areas, (5) inertia and household tenure, (6) informa-tion flows, (7) presence of friends and relatives at possible destina-tions, and (8) urban-rural amenity differentials. As any or all of these may interact with population growth and the land-tenure system to either stimulate or depress migration, an attempt has been made to include all those for which empirical measures could be ob-tained. Second, inclusion of other possible influences in the regres-sions aids evaluation of the relative importance of the central hy-potheses above and, subsequently, the import of the theoretical model. Third, although focus is on rural out-migration—mainly because rural-urban migration streams cannot be identified from census sources—inclusion of variables relating to provincial urban-rural differentials in wages and amenities enables some evaluation of the extent to which rural pushes dominate over urban pulls as causes of rural out-migration in Latin America.[9]

Conceptually there is a problem in determining whether the ur-ban pull comes from the same province as that in which the rural out-migration occurs and, therefore, whether an individual urban-rural differential measures that "pull." However, given the under-developed nature of rural labor markets, rural communications media, and rural transportation facilities in Latin America, and in view of a number of studies which suggest that large proportions of

9. A methodological shortcoming in the test is that it is not possible to evaluate the magnitude of the net influence of population growth effects and agrarian structure relative to other independent influences in rural emigration.

rural-urban migrants in Latin America are "stage migrants" (migrating from rural to small urban, to medium urban, and finally to large urban centers), it seems reasonable to assume that potential provincial rural migrants will perceive provincial urban wage and amenity differentials first and foremost.[10]

Income effects.—An established finding in migration research is that the magnitude of income differentials (i.e., income-earning possibilities) between places i and j is highly associated with the incidence and direction of migration between the two places. To evaluate the significance of income differentials, the regressions include both estimated wage levels in the area of origin as a possible push or retentive force and estimated urban-rural wage differentials.

In some cases it is open to question whether the wage estimates are representative for those vying for jobs in either the rural or urban labor markets. For example, in Chile the agricultural wage is represented by the average 1952-60 rural provincial economically active per capita agricultural gross domestic product. On the other hand, the urban-rural wage differential is represented by the average 1960 urban provincial economically active per capita manufacturing and services gross domestic product as a multiple of the same for agriculture. In the case of Peru, the 1940-61 wage and salary effect is represented by the 1961 median weekly agricultural worker's salary, whereas the urban-rural wage differential is represented by the 1961 median weekly manufacturing and service worker's salary as a multiple of the same for agriculture. In Costa Rica (1950-63) the agricultural wage effect and urban-rural differential is also estimated using 1958 agricultural, manufacturing, and service average salary data.

Another problem in using these estimates is the obvious time discrepancy between the period represented by the migration rates and the period represented by the wage estimates. In defense of their adequacy, one can only suggest that as agricultural conditions (that is, general income-earning prospects) have not varied much over the period of analysis in each country and as urban wage and income levels consistently demonstrate higher levels than agricultural wage and income levels (except in some Costa Rican provinces), the estimates should suffice as crude orders of magnitude. Hypotheses then are:

10. Admittedly, if this view is incorrect, the use of intraprovincial wage differentials to measure the strength of differential incomes as potential forces in migration would be open to question.

Hypothesis IIa—The higher the urban-rural provincial wage differential, the greater the incidence of provincial rural out-migration.

Hypothesis IIb—The higher the provincial agricultural wage, either the greater the incidence of rural out-migration as cost barriers assume less importance (assuming no relation between income and cost) *or the less the incidence of rural out-migration as retentive forces increase.*

Given current migration findings, it is difficult to state Hypothesis IIb in one direction only. For example, a premise of cost-benefit analysis when applied to migration is that as migration is costly (considering moving expenses, working time lost while migrating, and job seeking), a threshold income may be required to facilitate movement. On the other hand, higher agricultural wage levels would indicate greater opportunities in one province as against another. Also there may be difficulty in interpreting the regression results on this variable for Peru and the graphic analysis for Costa Rica, as the wage estimates are based on salary data, and salaried employees in the minifundio-latifundio complex represent a small proportion of the rural labor force.

Educational effects.—The extent to which a population is educated may influence migration behavior in three ways. First, in rural Latin America education may increase knowledge about different styles of life and income-earning possibilities in urban areas. Education also instills evaluative processes by which potential migrants may better perceive and evaluate alternative social and economic opportunities. Second, increased education may lead to a reluctance to accept traditional ways of agricultural life, especially if social and economic opportunities are suppressed by an inflexible social structure. Finally, levels of education may be an important factor in one's chances of getting a well-paid job in the city, that is, education increases the differential between opportunities in the rural community and the city.

As there is some evidence to suggest that extent of literacy in a population better reflects general capacities to perceive differential opportunities (by written communication, news media, etc.) than extent of schooling (that is, relating more to specific learned content), the measure of educational effects is taken to be average proportion of the rural male population illiterate.

Hypothesis III — The greater the extent of illiteracy in a provincial rural sector, the less the incidence of migration.

Differential amenities effects.—Amenity differentials between two areas may operate in a push-pull manner on the disadvantaged area. A common argument is that the "bright lights" of the city exert an important urban pull on potential rural migrants. Although it is difficult to operationalize the "bright lights" concept, measures of urban-rural differentials in availability and quality of housing, household facilities such as water and light, and availability of educational facilities for children have been included. There is a problem in interpreting these considerations, however, since the urban sector of each province invariably demonstrates a consistent advantage over the rural sector in terms of available amenities. Also, perception of these differentials is again likely to be dependent on both extent of education or literacy in the population and extent of urban-rural information flows about differential amenities. A third problem is that differential amenities are measured by single proxy variables, whereas potential migrants are most likely to consider the relative merits of "packages" of amenities evaluated in terms of such things as quantity, quality, or location. Nevertheless, a number of crude indicators relating to the quantity and quality of housing, urban-rural literacy differentials, and the extent of provincial urbanization (as a general "bright lights" indicator) are included in the quantitative analyses.

Hypothesis IVa—The greater the urban-rural differential in housing quality and facilities, the greater the urban pull on potential migrants and, consequently, *the greater the incidence of rural-urban migration* (testable for Peru and Costa Rica only).

Hypothesis IVb—The greater the urban-rural differential in availability of housing, the greater the urban pull on potential migrants in rural areas and, consequently, *the greater the incidence of provincial rural out-migration* (testable for Chile only).

Hypothesis IVc—The greater the urban-rural differential in literacy, the greater the urban pull on potential rural migrants and, consequently, *the greater the incidence of provincial rural out-migration.*

Hypothesis IVd—The greater the proportion of the provincial population located in urban centers, the greater the urban pull on potential rural migrants (that is, a gravity effect occurs) and, consequently, *the greater the incidence of provincial rural out-migration.*

Availability of transportation.—In the context of rural Latin America, it is very difficult to measure the extent to which inadequate means of transportation impede rural out-migration. Although distances must be considered, transportation of household items may not present a problem, as the rural-agricultural worker is not likely to have accumulated many material possessions.

On the other hand, the availability of a variety of means of transportation, such as cars, buses, and trains, may facilitate exploratory trips to alternative places of residence and information about opportunities elsewhere.[11] Only in the case of Chile are data available on means of transportation.

Hypothesis V—The greater the means of transportation available to the population of place i, the greater the incidence of migration out of the area (testable for Chile only).

As mentioned previously, it is important to keep in mind that although the various determinants of migration hypothesized above are posited as univariate relationships, their effects are not expected to be independent of one another. Rather, it is likely that the variety of influences discussed above interact to produce both pushes and pulls in the rural area of origin. In some cases, hypothesized influences such as the rural-urban wage differential will be not only associated with, but caused by, other hypothesized influences (i.e., conditions in agriculture). Accordingly, in the multiple-regression analysis of Chilean and Peruvian migration, interest is not only in evaluating the simple hypothesized relationships, but also in isolating those influences which interact to stimulate and/or depress rural out-migration.

STATISTICAL METHODOLOGY—SOME FINAL CONSIDERATIONS

Units of Analysis.—In both the application of the regression analysis and interpretation of the results, steps have been taken to

11. The distance factor does not play as significant a role in Chilean migration as one might expect given that the country spans some 3,000 miles. The correlation of

insure that the population composition of each unit of analysis is relatively homogeneous and that each unit of analysis has equal weight (i.e., importance) in a regression.

As noted previously, the criterion of relative homogeneity directs that only those provinces with at least 80 percent of their rural male labor force in agricultural occupations in the agricultural industry be included in the quantitative analysis. Accordingly, 15 of Chile's 25 provinces, 19 of Peru's 24 provinces, and 6 of Costa Rica's 7 provinces qualify. All Colombian provinces for which data were available qualify ($n = 12$).

To overcome differences in the relative size of the units of analysis (that is, the provinces) and, therefore, their representativeness in the regressions, a weighted regression analysis has also been performed for Chile and Peru. The rationale behind a weighted regression analysis is given in Appendix IV. Briefly, the problem is that when using rates as measures of the incidence of various characteristics in a population, observations on dependent and independent variables for each unit of analysis are given the same weight or importance in a regression. Yet there may be vast differences in the size of each unit of analysis and, therefore, in the relative importance of the rate (i.e., the incidence of migration) for the country as a whole. Given that the researcher may have no control over the size of the units of analysis for which data are available, he must make adjustments to insure that observations included in the regression are of equal significance relative to the size or importance of the populations they represent. Making an adjustment of this sort yields 37 units of analysis for Chile, 240 for Peru, and 15 for Costa Rica. For Chile and Peru, both unweighted and weighted regressions have been performed, and results compared. For Costa Rica and Colombia, the relative importance of the observations is conveyed in a graphic analysis.

Variable Measurement.—In the previous sections, some mention has already been made of problems associated with reliability of the data, problems of using proxy variables, unequal time references for dependent and independent variables, and incomparability of measures on independent variables between countries. We will elaborate briefly on each of these.

"distance" with rates of provincial out-migration to the province of Santiago yielded a coefficient of only $r = -0.47$, which failed to take on statistical significance in a multiple-regression analysis of the determinants of Chilean interprovincial population migration.

The principal source of data for each country is the national census of population and agriculture. Generally, cross-checking of statistics on population and labor-force characteristics, both within single census volumes and between separate publications, indicates that census publications of the 1950s and after are of reasonable quality. Although underenumeration, especially in rural areas, is an oft-cited problem and as means of correction are not available, it appears reasonable to assume that this error is evenly distributed among provinces.

Given either inadequate concepts for which empirical measures have as yet to be devised, or inadequate sources of data, the researcher is often forced to use proxy variables. Frequently the correspondence between the proxy and the theoretical construct for which the proxy variable has been devised is far from satisfactory. This is essentially an empirical problem; it is dependent upon both the resourcefulness of the researcher and the availability of suitable data.

Again, the necessity of using measures of dependent and independent variables which differ with respect to time reference is a result of inadequate data. For example, the rate of male labor-force provincial rural out-migration in Peru measures the incidence of migration over the time interval 1940-61. In contrast, most of the measures of provincial agricultural and population characteristics are for the year 1961, because the first national agricultural census of Peru was enumerated in 1961. The only means of reconciling this divergence is to assume that the measures of the provincial rural-agricultural and population characteristics represent typical orders of magnitude that have persisted over the previous decades. Given the slow pace by which social and economic change has been introduced into rural Latin America over the 1940-60 period, this assumption seems reasonable, although changes will have occurred resulting in an error factor of unknown importance.

Quantitative analysis is performed separately for each country for a number of reasons. First, data for empirical measures of the various hypothesized influences are not comparable between countries. Second, although the presence or absence of similar factors may dominate as causes of rural out-migration in different countries, lower and upper limits in the levels or magnitudes of rural out-migration may be dependent upon certain general characteristics of the country, such as its geographical topography, political organization, or degree of urbanization. For these reasons, observations for all provinces in the three countries have not been combined in one regression, although rural migration for each country as a whole is compared relative to national indexes of socioeconomic development.

Precautions in the Regression Analysis.—Given the small numbers of observations for the unweighted analysis of migration in Chile ($n = 15$) and Peru ($n = 19$) and, therefore, the small number of degrees of freedom, it is necessary to adjust the regression coefficient of multiple determination from R^2 to R^2_{adj}. Also, as the number of observations is small, the number of independent variables in the various regressions has also been kept small. Actually, every possible combination of independent variables has been examined.

Problems of multicollinearity are handled in two ways. First, only small numbers of independent variables are included in each regression. Second, it is not necessary to rely on typically vague interpretations of the extent to which a number of variables are collinear using only single correlation coefficients in a correlation coefficient matrix. Rather, the University of Pennsylvania's Bio-Medical Sciences regression program (BMDO3R) provides multicollinearity coefficients of determination in which regressions of independent variables included in a specific equation are performed on themselves. That is, in a regression with independent variables a, b, c, and d, regressions are also run on independent variable a as the dependent variable with variables b, c, and d acting as independent variables, and so forth. Accordingly, the Bio-Medical program tells us that multicollinearity is serious for particular independent-variable combinations when a collinearity coefficient of determination ($R^2_{a, b, c, d}$) exceeds 0.50. This is simply a warning light that sampling errors in individual coefficients become large and that regression coefficients are not very precisely estimated even though the overall correlation for the entire equation is high.

SUMMARY

The central concern in the quantitative analysis, then, is to evaluate both the absolute and relative importance of interactions in the rate of population increase and the land-tenure system as a causal force in the incidence of provincial rural out-migration. In keeping with the descriptive model, we would expect the measure incorporating both provincial population growth effects and the structure of the land-tenure system to be highly significant in accounting for variations in rural migration. The direction of the relationship is, of course, expected to be positive, rather than negative or inverse.

To consider both the absolute role and interaction of other likely determinants of migration, wage, education, and amenity differentials have been included. Where urban-rural wage or amenity differentials exist in favor of the urban areas, an urban pull effect has been hypothesized, with corresponding increases in the incidence of rural out-migration. On the other hand, as a lack of education, or illiteracy, is likely to have the effect of conditioning man's perception of differential opportunities and willingness to accept traditional forms of rural life, a negative relationship between these considerations and rural out-migration behavior has been hypothesized.

Using multiple-regression analysis for Chile and Peru and a graphic analysis for Costa Rica and Colombia, the determinants of provincial rural out-migration have been analyzed for each country separately. Between-country comparisons have been made largely at the national level and involve both comparisons of the migration experience in the three sample countries and the relationship between the structure of land tenure and rural out-migration in Latin America in general.

4. Empirical Results

A S A FIRST indication of the degree of association between the principal independent variables and the provincial rate of rural male labor-force out-migration in Chile, consider the simple correlation coefficients in Table 4.1. Clearly, the variables reflecting provincial differences in the land-tenure system and population growth demonstrate the highest degree of association with our dependent variable M_C. With the exception of the urban-rural housing differential (C_{10}), marginal or insignificant relationships appear between the variables and M_C.[1] Although the coefficients in Table 4.1 are for unweighted observations ($n = 15$), the coefficients for a weighted analysis ($n = 37$) are almost identical. (See Appendix V for independent-variable values and sources.)

In the majority of cases, the signs of the simple correlation coefficients are in keeping with the hypotheses. With respect to Hypothesis IIb concerning the possibility of either a positive or negative

---

1. It has been brought to the author's attention that the 1960 Chilean data on housing are dubious, since 1960 was the year of the big earthquake, with many houses being destroyed in some of the southern provinces. On the other hand, the period 1952-59 was nearly earthquake-free. Apparently, local officials were all too eager to add "substandard" housing to that actually destroyed by the earthquake, raising their figures for the overall housing "shortage" in hopes of receiving more relief funds.

Table 4.1. Simple Correlation Coefficients for the Independent Variables and M_C

	(a) Simple Correlation Coefficient r	(b) Student t for (a)

Dependent Variable

M_C = 1952–60 provincial rural male labor-force out-migrants per 100 average 1952–60 provincial rural male labor force

Independent Variables

A. Structure of agriculture

	(a)	(b)
C_1 = % of provincial farm holdings having <5 hectares (minifundios), 1955	0.52	2.14[a]
C_2 = % of provincial agricultural land held by farms >500 hectares (latifundios), 1955	0.67	3.26[b]
C_3 = % of provincial agricultural labor force on farms <5 hectares weighted by average provincial population growth rates, 1952–60	0.77	4.28[b]
C_4 = Average % of provincial agricultural labor-force employees and productive workers, 1952–60	0.34	1.34

B. Population pressure on land

	(a)	(b)
C_{5a} = Stock index of provincial rural population pressure and agricultural inopportunity, 1952	0.84	5.40[b]
C_{5b} = Flow index of provincial rural population pressure and agricultural inopportunity, 1952–60	0.88	6.25[b]

C. Income effects

C_6 = Average provincial agricultural wage, 1952–60	0.51	2.15[a]
C_7 = % change in provincial agricultural wage, 1952–60	−0.001	−0.003
C_8 = Average provincial urban wage index as a multiple of average provincial rural wage index, 1960	−0.06	0.21

D. Education

C_9 = Average % of provincial rural male population illiterate, 1952–60	−0.36	1.40

E. Differential amenities effect

C_{10} = Provincial urban housing shortage per 100 urban population as a multiple of rural provincial housing shortage per 100 rural population, 1960	−0.74	4.00[b]
C_{11} = Average % of provincial urban population literate as a multiple of average % of provincial rural population literate, 1952–60	−0.29	−1.10
C_{12} = Average % of provincial population classified as urban, 1952–60	0.31	1.18

F. Availability of transportation

C_{13} = Number of cars, buses, and trucks per 1,000 provincial population, 1960	0.49	2.05[a]

a. Significant at the 0.05 level.

b. Significant at the 0.01 level.

effect of higher provincial average agricultural wage and salary levels on rural migration, the correlation coefficient assumed a statistically significant positive sign. This suggests that higher wage levels, as a proxy for higher levels of household income, reduce cost barriers to migration. Another interpretation is that where agricultural wages or salaries are high, urban opportunities are likely to be handily present and would thus act to attract potential rural out-migrants.[2]

With respect to the general relevance of the model, Table 4.1 also indicates something about the importance of considering both the stock and flow of population and labor demands on the land. For example, in the correlation between M_C and the proportion of the provincial farm holdings less than 5 hectares, P_1 (i.e., $r = 0.52$), we considered only one aspect of the structure of land tenure, that is, a proportion of the rural population with a specifically limited range of income-earning opportunities and their stock of demands on the land. By introducing provincial population growth rates, we also take into consideration the flow of population and labor-force demands within the minifundio class (C_3).[3] Considering both stocks and flows in this manner increases the degree of association between these "indexes of provincial agricultural inopportunity" and M_C almost 1-1/2 times ($r = 0.77$). An extension of this approach, of course, has been to incorporate the effects of latifundio landholding and the large pool of agricultural employees and production workers not employed on latifundios. These act as further "conditioners" of both the stock and flow of population and labor-force demands on the land and the land available to the majority of the rural-agricultural labor force.

In defense of the stock and flow derivations over simpler measures, Table 4.2 presents coefficients of determination for the dependent variable M_C and a number of variations on the stock index. Index 4, a typical population pressure measure used in demographic studies, largely ignores production possibilities (e.g., arable agricultural land actually available for cultivation by the majority of the population), as well as which population subgroups rely more than others upon arable land as a source of livelihood. Replacing the numerator in index 4 with T_A (provincial arable land) improves the

2. A correlation-coefficient matrix is presented in Table 4.4.

3. Though not reported in Table 4.1, provincial rates of population growth and simple population density measures had low and statistically insignificant correlation coefficients with the measure of out-migration. This result held for Peru and Costa Rica.

"predictive" import of index 3. In support of the argument in Chapter 2 that latifundismo seriously restricts the production possibilities of the rural population in general, index 2, incorporating L_A, accounts for approximately 10 percent more of the variation in M_C. Thus, results for index 2, more than those for index 3, support Hypothesis Id pertaining to the role of latifundismo in rural out-migration. Finally, including the component $f(L_0 + L_w + F_0)$ in the index (index 1) tends to support the assumption that this rural population subgroup is not experiencing the same income-producing problems as the population at large and therefore should be excluded from the measures of population pressure.

Table 4.2. Simple Linear Regression Results for M_C and Variations on the Stock Index of Population Pressure and Agricultural Inopportunity

		Dependent Variable M_C
Index	Population Pressure Measure	r^2_{adj}
1	$\left[P_t - f(L_0 + L_w + F_0) \right] / (T_A - L_A)$	0.70
2	$P_t / (T_A - L_A)$	0.65
3	P_t / T_A	0.55
4	$P_t /$ (total nonsterile agricultural land)	0.13

Generally, the results in Table 4.2 were the same for the flow index. Excluding growth in the component $f(L_0 + L_w + F_0)$ from time t to $t + n$, thereby resulting in a flow index of $[P_t(1 + r)^n - P_t] / (T_A - L_A)$, resulted in an $r^2 = 0.68$. Including growth in the component $f(L_0 + L_w + F_0)$ enabled the flow index to account for approximately 2 percent more variation, $r^2_{adj} = 0.72$.

Clearly, the "predictive" capacity of both the stock and flow indexes is very close. This indicates that the flow is generally proportional to the stock and that although rates of population natural increase vary between provinces, the variations neither are large enough nor operate long enough during the study period to distort the close correlation between the two measures (the correlation of C_{5a} and C_{5b} is $r = 0.95$).

Given that the stock and flow measures are highly correlated and that in all of the regressions performed, each index demonstrated approximately the same "predictive" capacity, the stock index C_{5a} is represented as the basic predictor in each of the regressions.[4]

To evaluate income effects on provincial rural migration, the first multiple-regression equation (equation 1) illustrates the dominance of the index of population pressure and agricultural inopportunity in contrast to three wage variables: the average provincial agricultural wage, C_6; the percentage change in the provincial average agricultural wage 1952-60, C_7; and the urban-rural wage differential, C_8.

$$(\text{Eq. 1}) \quad M_C = 2.91 + 2.70C_{5a} - 0.0005\ C_6 - 0.012C_7 - 0.234C_8$$
$$\phantom{(\text{Eq. 1}) \quad M_C =} (0.425) \quad (0.018) \quad\quad (0.032) \quad\quad (0.420)$$
$$R^2 = 0.73 \quad R^2\text{adj} = 0.65 \quad F\ \text{ratio} = 12.51.$$

Directly beneath each regression coefficient, standard errors of the regression coefficients have been placed in parentheses, the coefficients of determination are presented both unadjusted and adjusted (for the small number of degrees of freedom), and an overall F ratio for the $R^2\text{adj}$ is given. In Table 4.3, partial correlation coefficients, Student t values, and multicollinearity coefficients of determination are provided.

Clearly, C_{5a} demonstrates the highest "explanatory" utility whereas the wage variables are all statistically insignificant (see Table 4.3), and account for only 1 percent of the variation in M_C. However, on the grounds of this finding, it is not to be implied that income-producing possibilities in the area of origin (or in contrast to alternative places of residence) are not important in decisions to migrate. Possibly, the measures of wage and salary differentials are not representative of those which confront the minifundio and landless employee class. On the other hand, if the description of conditions within the minifundio-latifundio complex is accurate, the stock index (or flow index) should better represent the complex of factors determining rural income-earning possibilities than a traditional wage or rural-urban wage differential variable.

In all other regressions involving the stock index, similar results

4. As against using C_{5a} (or C_{5b}) as an overall index of population pressure, an investigation was made of the predictive capacity of linear combinations of simpler variables which are included in C_{5a}. For example, multiple regressions including index 3 or P_t/T_A (as in Table 4.2) with C_2, C_2 and C_3, C_2 and C_3 and C_4, etc., were tried. In each case, however, multicollinearity between these independent variables was a serious problem and in no case did the predictive capacity parallel that of the overall stock or flow index (i.e., an r^2 value of at least 10 percent less).

Table 4.3. Partial Correlation Coefficients, Student t Values, Proportion of Variance Cumulated, and Collinearity Coefficients of Determination for Regression Equations--Chile

Equation	Variable	Partial Correlation Coefficient	Student t Values	Proportion of Variance Cumulated	Collinearity Coefficients of Determination
1	$C_{5\alpha}$	0.83	6.37[a]	0.730	$C_{5\alpha} \cdot 7,8,6 = 0.3982$
	C_7	-0.11	-0.37	0.005	$C_7 \cdot 5\alpha,8,6 = 0.4584$
	C_8	-0.17	-0.56	0.006	$C_8 \cdot 5\alpha,7,6 = 0.4437$
	C_6	-0.26	-0.04	0.000	$C_6 \cdot 5\alpha,7,8 = 0.3976$
2	C_8	0.07	0.22	0.000	$C_8 \cdot 10,11 = 0.0300$
	C_{10}	-0.72	-3.40[a]	0.469	$C_{10} \cdot 8,11 = 0.1497$
	C_{11}	-0.03	-0.08	0.085	$C_{11} \cdot 8,10 = 0.1529$
3	C_6	0.54	2.24[a]	0.203	$C_6 \cdot 12 = 0.0002$
	C_{12}	0.40	1.51	0.177	
4	$C_{5\alpha}$	0.84	5.40[a]	0.742	

a. Significant at the 0.01 level.

have been obtained: that is, C_{5a} totally dominates as the "explanatory" variable while the additional variables are usually both of the "wrong" sign and statistically insignificant. Even when C_{5a} is combined with the relatively strong urban-rural housing shortage differential C_{10}, this variable also assumes the unexpected sign and is statistically insignificant. Although this finding may seem unusual as the two variables do not appear to be interrelated, they are actually highly collinear. From the correlation coefficient matrix presented in Table 4.4, we find a correlation coefficient of -0.85 between C_{5a} and C_{10}. This means that an increase in rural population pressure is likely to be associated with an increase in the rural housing shortage and therefore a decline in the ratio of the urban-rural housing shortage, C_{10}.

On the other hand, exclusion of C_{5a} from a number of regressions does result in the expected signs for variables which were originally moderately correlated with M_C. For example, in equation 2, three amenity variables relating to urban-rural differentials in housing shortages (C_{10}), literacy (C_{11}), and wages (C_8) all carry expected signs though only C_{10} is statistically significant:

(Eq 2) $M_C = 15.37 + 0.136C_8 - 1.23C_{10} - 0.609C_{11}$
$\qquad\qquad\qquad (0.599) \quad\ (0.361) \quad\ (7.376)$
$\qquad\qquad\quad R^2 = 0.55 \quad R^2\text{adj} = 0.39 \quad F \text{ ratio} = 4.56.$

Another combination of interest includes a measure of urbanization, C_{12}, and the provincial average agricultural wage, C_6, as in equation 3:

(Eq. 3) $M_C = 8.51 + 0.108C_6 + 0.063C_{12}$
$\qquad\qquad\qquad (0.048) \quad\ (0.042)$
$\qquad\qquad\quad R^2 = 0.38 \quad R^2\text{adj} = 0.23 \quad F \text{ ratio} = 3.69.$

Both variables retain signs consistent with the hypotheses and are statistically significant. Their overall utility for predicting variations in M_C, however, is low.

Concluding, the stock index of population pressure and agricultural inopportunity dominates each regression and the equation providing the best fit is simply

(Eq. 4) $M_C = 0.429 + 2.51C_{5a}$
$\qquad\qquad\qquad\ (0.367)$
$\qquad\quad r^2 = 0.74 \quad r^2\text{adj} = 0.70 \quad F \text{ ratio} = 46.7.$

In the table of residuals presented in Table 4.5, actual values for M_C and regression estimates are given for both an unweighted and a weighted equation 4. Generally, the range of deviations lies between 10 and 40 percent in the unweighted analysis and is nar-

Table 4.4. -Correlation Coefficient Matrix of Major Independent Variables--Chile

	C_1	C_2	C_3	C_4	C_5	C_6	C_7	C_8	C_9	C_{10}	C_{11}	C_{12}	C_{13}
C_1	1.000	0.667	0.985	0.754	0.859	0.333	0.419	0.100	-0.245	-0.703	-0.087	0.460	0.340
C_2		1.000	0.673	0.373	0.535	0.067	0.475	0.418	-0.224	-0.473	-0.097	0.381	0.274
C_3			1.000	0.745	0.899	0.396	0.346	0.073	-0.289	-0.772	-0.115	0.489	0.644
C_4				1.000	0.551	0.016	0.358	-0.266	0.040	-0.471	-0.152	0.300	0.338
C_5					1.000	0.639	0.082	0.039	-0.560	-0.849	-0.406	0.588	0.862
C_6						1.000	-0.456	0.129	-0.690	-0.688	-0.402	0.733	-0.080
C_7							1.000	0.234	0.220	0.156	0.141	-0.186	0.014
C_8								1.000	-0.081	0.137	0.150	0.378	0.063
C_9									1.000	0.569	0.893	-0.581	-0.684
C_{10}										1.000	0.387	-0.570	0.690
C_{11}											1.000	-0.212	-0.230
C_{12}												1.000	0.552
C_{13}													1.000

rowed somewhat in the weighted analysis. As a general indicant of dispersion we find that in the unweighted analysis 86.1 percent of the regression estimates had deviations of less than 50 percent, whereas in the weighted analysis all estimates had deviations of less than 50 percent.

The most significant deviation is for the province of Santiago (51 percent overestimated for the unweighted regression and 32 percent for the weighted regression), which constitutes 13.9 percent of the sample rural population. In this case, it is likely that the stock index of population pressure and agricultural inopportunity does not adequately reflect rural income-earning opportunities in Santiago. For example, a combination of (1) the highest provincial agricultural wage and (2) off-farm income-earning opportunities given that approximately 90 percent of the provincial population is urban, may tend to dampen the pressure resulting from population growth and lack of opportunity within the minifundio-latifundio complex. A clue that this interpretation is correct lies in a comparison of the migration experience of Santiago with that of Valparaíso. In Valparaíso, the rate of out-migration is higher as is the value for the stock and flow indexes of population pressure (see Appendix V). However, as in the case of Santiago, out-migration is overestimated by equation 4. Again, however, Valparaíso has almost as high an agricultural wage and almost as large an urban proportion of its population. All of the remaining variables for the two provinces are similar except that Valparaíso had an increase in its agricultural wage from 1952 to 1960 which was offset by a high urban-rural wage differential. As for the remaining cases with a sizable overestimate (for example, Osorno and Bío-Bío) or underestimate (such as Malleco), it is difficult to identify underlying similarities.

PERU

The simple correlation coefficients presented in Table 4.6 indicate that in Peru the system of land tenure is also an important influence in provincial rural out-migration.[5] [As in the case of Chile, although these coefficients are for unweighted observations ($n = 19$), the coefficients for a weighted analysis are almost identical.] The stock and flow indexes, P_{5a} and P_{5b}, clearly demonstrate the strongest relationship with Mp although they are not as significant as in the

5. A correlation-coefficient matrix is provided in Table 4.9.

Table 4.5 Residuals for Weighted and Unweighted Regression Analysis in Equation 4—Chile

Province	Actual[a]	Unweighted Estimate	Weighted Estimate	Unweighted Deviation	Weighted Deviation	% Unweighted Deviation	% Weighted Deviation	Proportion of Sample Population Represented
Aconcagua	13.10	11.10	10.68	-1.99	-2.42	15.3	18.4	4.1
Valparaíso	7.90	9.38	9.06	1.48	1.16	19.6	14.7	4.2
Santiago	5.50	7.82	7.59	2.32	2.09	51.1	37.0	13.9
O'Higgins	10.40	8.96	8.68	-1.42	-1.72	13.6	15.6	7.4
Colchagua	6.00	5.96	5.84	-0.04	-0.16	0.6	2.7	6.1
Curicó	3.60	4.59	4.55	0.99	0.95	28.0	26.4	3.4
Talca	3.20	3.78	3.79	0.58	0.59	18.1	18.4	6.4
Maule	4.00	3.19	3.24	-0.81	-0.79	20.0	19.0	2.7
Linares	4.10	4.67	4.63	0.57	0.53	14.0	13.0	6.2
Ñuble	4.10	3.51	3.54	-0.61	-0.56	15.0	13.6	9.8
Bío-Bío	2.40	3.43	3.46	1.03	1.06	43.0	44.1	5.8
Malleco	6.00	3.18	3.24	-2.82	-2.76	47.0	46.0	5.7
Cautín	3.40	3.16	3.21	-0.24	-0.19	7.0	5.6	14.1
Osorno	3.50	4.83	4.78	1.33	1.28	37.8	36.5	4.4
Llanquihue	5.00	4.62	4.58	-0.38	-0.42	7.6	8.4	5.6

a. All rates of rural out-migration are expressed as positive. If, overall, net rural in-migration is experienced, the rate is represented as negative.

Note: The proportion of the total sample population for which deviations were less than 50 percent was, for the unweighted regression, 86.1 percent, and for the weighted regression, 100.0 percent.

Table 4.6. Simple Correlation Coefficients for the Independent Variables and M_P

	(a) Simple Correlation Coefficient r	(b) Student t for (a)
Dependent Variable		
M_P = 1940–61 provincial rural male labor-force out-migrants per 100 average 1940–61 provincial rural male labor-force		
Independent Variables		
A. Structure of agriculture		
P_1 = % of provincial farm holdings having <5 hectares (minifundios), 1961	0.35	1.36
P_2 = % of provincial agricultural land held by farms in excess of 500 hectares (latifundios), 1961	0.64	3.50[a]
P_3 = % of provincial agricultural labor force on minifundios weighted by average provincial population growth rates, 1940–61	0.61	3.16[a]
P_4 = % of provincial agricultural labor-force employees and productive workers, 1961	0.26	1.09
B. Population pressure on land		
P_{5a} = Stock index of provincial rural population pressure and agricultural inopportunity, 1940–61	0.72	4.03[a]
P_{5b} = Flow index of provincial rural population pressure and agricultural inopportunity, 1940–61	0.75	4.14[a]

C. Income effects

P_6 = Provincial median weekly agricultural workers salary, 1961   0.26   1.13

P_7 = Provincial median urban salary as a multiple of provincial median rural salary, 1961   0.17   0.72

D. Education

P_8 = % of provincial rural male population aged 15 years and over illiterate, 1961   -0.03   -0.14

E. Differential amenities effect

P_9 = Index of provincial urban housing quality as a multiple of provincial rural housing quality, 1961   -0.19   -0.82

P_{10} = Average % of provincial urban population literate as a multiple of % of provincial rural population literate, 1940–61   -0.03   -0.14

P_{11} = Average % of provincial population classified as urban, 1940–61   0.20   0.84

a. Significant at the 0.01 level.

Chilean context.[6] With respect to considering both the stock and flow of population and labor-force demands on the land, the correlation coefficients for P_1 through P_4 further indicate the importance of taking both effects into consideration.

Again, in support of our stock and flow measures over simpler derivations, Table 4.7 presents coefficients of determination for the dependent variable Mp and a number of variations on the stock index.

Table 4.7. Simple Linear Regression Results for M_p and Variations on the Stock Index of Population Pressure and Agricultural Inopportunity

		Dependent Variable M_p
Index	Population Pressure Measure	r^2 adj
1	$P_t - f(L_O + F_O) \, / \, (T_A - L_A)$	0.50
2	$P_t \, / \, (T_A - L_A)$	0.44
3	$P_t \, / \, T_A$	0.04
4	$P_t \, /$ (total nonsterile agricultural land)	0.00

Clearly, the Peruvian case attests to the importance of taking into consideration the role of latifundismo in the distribution of land and subgroups that are not likely to experience situations of economic stress, that is, $f(L_O + F_O)$. The reason that the L_A factor influences the "predictive" capacity of index 2 (as against index 1) to a much greater extent in Peru than in Chile is the greater variation between Peruvian provinces in the holdings of arable land by latifundios. Again, Hypothesis Id is corroborated and the frequently used measure of population to total agricultural land is of no predictive value whatsoever.

As in the case of Chile, the magnitudes in Table 4.2 are similar for

6. Due to data limitations, the index of population pressure and agricultural inopportunity for Peru is not identical to that for Chile. The discrepancy lies in the numerator and the population subgroups taken into consideration (among others, latifundio workers and their dependents and owners of medium-sized farms and their dependents). In the Peruvian indexes of population pressure and agricultural inopportunity, data are not available for workers on latifundios. Therefore, the numerator only includes latifundistas and their dependents and operators of farms sized 5-500 hectares and their dependents.

Table 4.8. Partial Correlation Coefficients, Student t Values, Proportion of Variance Cumulated, and Collinearity Coefficients of Determination for Regression Equations--Peru

Equation	Variable	Partial Correlation Coefficient	Student t Values	Proportion of Variance Cumulated	Collinearity Coefficients of Determination
5	P_{5a}	0.77	4.59[a]	0.552	$P_{5a} \cdot 6,7 = 0.0962$
	P_6	0.07	0.29	0.010	$P_6 \cdot 5a,7 = 0.1299$
	P_7	0.42	1.77[b]	0.078	$P_7 \cdot 5a,6 = 0.0510$
6	P_7	0.14	0.56	0.020	$P_7 \cdot 10,9 = 0.0790$
	P_9	-0.20	-0.80	0.040	$P_9 \cdot 7,10 = 0.0630$
	P_{10}	-0.10	-0.39	0.000	$P_{10} \cdot 7,9 = 0.1310$
7	P_{5a}	0.81	5.45[a]	0.489	$P_5 \cdot 11 = 0.0781$
	P_{11}	0.59	2.90[c]	0.176	

a. Significant at the 0.01 level.

b. Significant at the 0.10 level.

c. Significant at the 0.05 level.

the flow index. For example, excluding growth of the component $f(L_0 + F_0)$ from the flow index results in $r^2 = 0.49$ or approximately 4 percent less than for the full measure, $r^2 = 0.53$.

For the remaining variables, most of the signs of the simple correlation coefficients are in keeping with the hypotheses though all fail to be statistically significant. Again, with respect to Hypothesis IIb concerning the possibility of either a positive or negative effect of higher provincial agricultural income levels (P_6) and rural migration (Mp), the correlation coefficient assumes a positive sign although it is not statistically significant.

Again, as the stock and flow indexes are closely correlated, P_{5a} is represented as the basic predictor in each of the regressions.[7] The first multiple-regression equation (equation 5) combines P_{5a} with two wage variables, the provincial median agricultural salary, P_6, and the urban-rural salary differential, P_7:

(Eq. 5) $Mp = -3.176 + 2.499P_{5a} + 0.006P_6 + 1.60P_7$
$\qquad\qquad\quad (0.544) \qquad (0.021) \qquad (1.77)$
$\qquad\qquad R^2 = 0.64 \qquad R^2_{adj} = 0.55 \quad F\ ratio = 8.6.$

All variables demonstrate signs consistent with the hypotheses although P_6 is not statistically significant and P_7 is barely significant at the 0.10 level. In Table 4.8, P_6 and P_7 combined account for only 8 percent of the cumulative variance whereas P_{5a} accounts for 55 percent.

As revealed in equation 6, provincial urban-rural amenity differentials appear to exert little influence on the incidence of rural out-migration. All variables are statistically insignificant with only P_7 demonstrating the expected sign:

(Eq. 6) $Mp = 8.58 + 1.24P_7 - 1.61P_9 - 0.736P_{10}$
$\qquad\qquad\qquad (2.22) \qquad (1.99) \qquad (1.867)$
$\qquad\quad R^2 = 0.061 \qquad R^2_{adj} = -0.189 \quad F\ ratio = 0.64.$

The only other regression in which the variables demonstrate consistency of sign and statistical significance include P_{5a} and our measure of the provincial urban population, P_{11}. In equation 7, then, P_{11} accounts for approximately 17 percent of the cumulated variance (see Table 4.8) whereas P_{5a} accounts for approximately 50 percent of the variance:

7. As in the case of Chile, combinations of simpler variables—as against the overall stock or flow indexes of population pressure—have also been run in multiple regressions. Again, however, the regressions have been plagued by problems of multicollinearity and the r^2 values have always been inferior to those obtained for P_{5a} (at least by 20 percent).

Table 4.9. Correlation Coefficient Matrix of Major Independent Variables—Peru

	P_1	P_2	P_3	P_4	P_5	P_6	P_7	P_8	P_9	P_{10}	P_{11}
P_1	1.000	0.847	0.536	-0.003	0.502	-0.108	0.089	0.219	-0.708	0.340	0.212
P_2		1.000	0.529	0.197	0.746	0.089	0.014	0.021	-0.549	0.230	0.113
P_3			1.000	0.472	0.692	0.419	0.075	-0.075	-0.417	-0.077	0.064
P_4				1.000	0.258	0.600	-0.260	-0.492	0.047	-0.490	0.613
P_5					1.000	-0.217	0.216	0.184	-0.168	0.336	-0.097
P_6						1.000	-0.229	-0.718	0.036	-0.783	0.727
P_7							1.000	0.348	-0.083	0.281	0.442
P_8								1.000	-0.082	0.596	-0.654
P_9									1.000	-0.251	0.354
P_{10}										1.000	0.621
P_{11}											1.000

(Eq. 7) $Mp = -4.976 + 2.123P_{5a} + 0.106P_{11}$
$$(0.389) \qquad (0.037)$$
$$R^2 = 0.67 \qquad R^2{}_{adj} = 0.60 \qquad F \text{ ratio} = 16.00.$$

With an $R^2{}_{adj}$ of 0.60, equation 7 provides the best-fit regression line accounting for variations in Peruvian provincial rural migration behavior. Table 4.9 presents a correlation coefficient matrix and Table 4.10 presents the residuals for equation 7, both unweighted and weighted.

Although the weighted regression narrows the provincial deviations considerably (Table 4.10), it is clear that we have not been as successful in accounting for provincial rural out-migration in Peru as in Chile. A look at individual cases, however, provides clues as to why the regression estimates (based largely on the stock index of population pressure and agricultural inopportunity) sometimes result in wide deviations. For example, in considering the overestimate for the province of Lima, a similar situation prevails as in the Chilean provinces of Santiago and Valparaíso. That is, Lima has the highest average agricultural wage in Peru and a large urban sector (81 percent) which may provide significant off-farm employment opportunities for those encountering situations of economic stress strictly within the minifundio-latifundio complex. In the province of Puno, there is also a significant overestimate, yet the magnitude of the urban sectors in these provinces (approximately 15 percent) suggests that not only may off-farm income opportunities not be available, but few urban employment prospects may confront those considering migration. On the other hand, for the provinces of Tacna and Huancavelica, there are significant underestimates of rural-urban migration. In the province of Tacna, greater than expected rural-urban migration (on the basis of equation 7) could be a function of the relatively high degree of urbanization, the relatively high urban-rural salary differential, and special government spending on an elaborate urban hospital and other facilities.

From a policy point of view, however, most of the largest percentage deviations in Table 4.10 (weighted analysis) are the least significant. That is, the largest discrepancies between actual and estimated Mp are for those provinces with the smallest rates of migration, generally representing a very small proportion of the total sample population. In fact, the two greatest percentage deviations are for provinces with net rates of rural in-migration (representing only 8.8 percent of the sample population). On the other hand, for approximately 85 percent of the population in the sample, the range of

Northland College
Dexter Library
Ashland, WI 54806

Table 4.10. Residuals for Weighted and Unweighted Regression Analysis in Equation 7--Peru

Province	Actual[a]	Unweighted Estimate	Weighted Estimate	Unweighted Deviation	Weighted Deviation	% Unweighted Deviation	% Weighted Deviation	Proportion of Sample Population
Tumbes	11.50	10.43	12.02	-1.07	0.56	9.3	-4.9	0.4
Piura	11.20	10.81	12.24	-0.39	1.43	3.5	12.7	7.2
Cajamarca	1.70	1.87	1.80	0.17	0.10	10.0	6.0	12.2
Lambayeque	11.30	12.03	12.22	0.73	0.83	6.8	7.3	2.5
La Libertad	11.00	9.26	9.41	-1.74	-1.58	15.8	14.3	6.8
Ancash	9.70	5.24	5.12	-4.44	-4.58	46.0	47.2	8.2
Huánuco	-1.20	2.03	1.93	3.23	3.13	268.0	260.0	5.1
Junín	10.10	7.04	6.74	-3.06	-3.36	35.7	33.2	5.5
Lima	5.40	9.44	7.77	4.04	2.37	74.1	44.0	5.3
Ica	2.50	3.54	3.29	1.04	0.79	41.6	31.8	2.2
Huancavelica	4.20	2.60	2.64	-1.60	-1.56	38.1	37.1	5.2
Ayacucho	3.80	4.02	3.13	0.22	-0.67	5.9	17.6	6.7
Cuzco	6.70	8.92	7.31	2.22	0.61	30.8	9.1	9.1
Apurímac	9.20	10.22	8.80	1.02	-0.39	11.1	4.3	5.2
Puno	6.80	10.49	8.80	3.89	2.03	57.2	30.0	12.4
Moquegua	12.10	7.37	6.41	-4.73	-5.69	39.1	47.0	0.6
Tacna	8.40	6.03	4.55	-2.37	-3.85	28.0	46.0	0.4
Loreto	-2.30	0.72	1.20	3.02	3.50	131.2	152.2	3.7
San Martín	2.40	2.41	1.64	0.01	-0.76	0.0	33.1	1.2

a. All rates of rural out-migration are expressed as positive. If, overall, net rural in-migration is experienced, the rate is expressed as negative.

Notes: The proportion of the total sample population for which deviations were less than 50 percent was, for the unweighted regression, 73.5 percent, and for the weighted regression, 91.2 percent.

Figure 4.1. Select Social and Economic Indicators and Migration in
Costa Rica, 1950-63

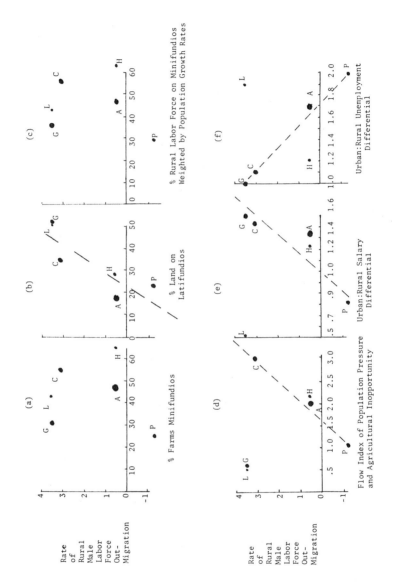

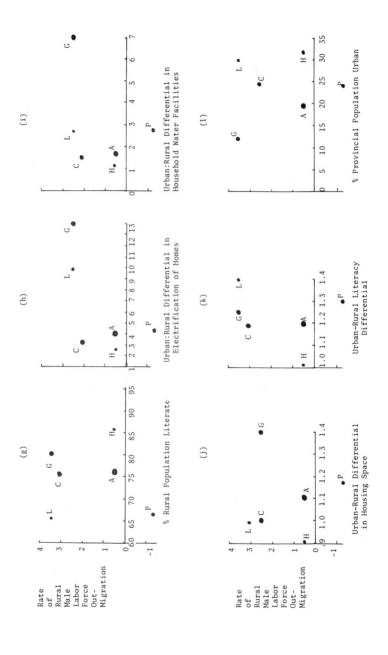

(g)

(h)

(i)

(j)

(k)

(l)

% Rural Population Literate

Urban:Rural Differential in
Electrification of Homes

Urban:Rural Differential in
Household Water Facilities

Urban-Rural Differential
in Housing Space

Urban-Rural Literacy
Differential

% Provincial Population Urban

Rate
of
Rural
Male
Labor
Force
Out-
Migration

deviations is on the same order as for Chile, between 10 and 40 percent.

COSTA RICA

Heeding the obvious limitations of a small number of observations (i.e., $n = 6$), variations in provincial net rates of rural male labor-force migration (M_{CR}) are evaluated in terms of a range of social, economic, and demographic indicators similar to those in the Chilean and Peruvian analyses. In Figure 4.1, relationships between the measure of migration and twelve independent variables are graphed separately. In each graph, values for the provinces are represented by a dot which is labeled by the first letter of the province.[8] The size of the dot indicates the relative size of the population in each province. In those cases in which a relationship is indicated, a simple linear regression line is conjectured.

Although the distribution of land to labor resources is considerably less uneven in Costa Rica than in either Chile or Peru, some provinces have relatively large proportions of their populations centralized on minifundios as well as relatively large tracts of land on latifundios.[9] To some extent, Figure 4.1a-d indicates a direct relationship between increasing rates of rural out-migration and measures of the distribution of labor to land resources. This is evident in part b where, as in the case of Chile and Peru, an increase in the proportion of the land held by latifundistas is more closely associated with M_{CR} than an increase in the proportion of the farms that are minifundios (as in Figure 4.1a). Unlike Chile and Peru, additional agricultural data for Costa Rica indicate that the proportion of the provincial farms that are minifundios may not be indicative of a general condition of agricultural inopportunity. For example, in Figure 4.1a, note the relatively low rate of out-migration for Heredia with 65 percent of its farms minifundios and the highest provincial rates of out-migration for the provinces of Guanacaste and Limón with only 30-40 percent of their farms minifundios. Yet additional agricultural statistics also indicate that the highest pro-

8. In Figure 4.1, the letters in the graphs representing provinces are: A = Alajuela, C = Cartago, H = Heredia, G = Guanacaste, P = Puntarenas, and L = Limón.

9. In Costa Rica, a minifundio is defined as a farm holding of less than 7 hectares and a latifundio as a farm holding in excess of 700 hectares. A range of 5-500 is not feasible as in the case of Chile and Peru, given the Costa Rican Census of Agriculture classifications.

portion of minifundios using fertilizer and irrigation methods is located in Heredia whereas in Guanacaste and Limón these forms of technology are barely in use on minifundios. The implication is that means for improving income-earning possibilities in the minifundio class are evident in Heredia, but not in Guanacaste or Limón.

Turning to Figure 4.1d, the flow index of population pressure and agricultural inopportunity indicates a relationship with M_{CR} for four provinces comprising 74.5 percent of the sample population. Again, the provinces of Guanacaste and Limón deviate widely. The extent of this relationship is the same for both the stock and flow indexes. (As in the case of Chile, all data are available for our stock and flow indexes.) On the other hand, unlike Chile and Peru, exclusion of the component $f(L_0 + L_w + F_0)$ from the numerator of the stock or flow index (or L_A from the denominator) does not affect the relationship indicated in Figure 4.1d to a great extent. In the latter case, the reason is that relatively small proportions of provincial arable land are held as latifundios. Where this is not the case, as in the province of Limón, a large number of workers are found on latifundios, indicating that latifundismo does not influence income-earning opportunities in Costa Rica in the same way as it does in Chile and Peru.

Although it is difficult to explain the high rate of migration in the province of Limón (only 6.7 percent of the sample population), Figure 4.1e-l indicates that a number of extraordinary influences are operating to stimulate relatively high rates of out-migration in the province of Guanacaste. For example, Guanacaste's urban-rural salary differential is the highest in the country (Figure 4.1e), the urban-rural unemployment differential is lowest (Figure 4.1f), the average proportion of rural literate is among the highest (Figure 4.1g), and the province has the highest urban-rural amenity differentials including higher literacy, greater urban electrification of homes (Figure 4.1h), more water facilities in homes (Figure 4.1i), and more housing space (Figure 4.1j). Accordingly, were it possible to remove the province of Guanacaste from the analysis, it would seem reasonable to argue that the provincial system of land tenure in combination with population growth rates is of some influence in provincial variations in rural migration behavior. That this influence is limited, however, is also evident when the simpler measure of population to arable land is correlated with M_{CR}, revealing almost as close a relationship. Of course, this finding comes as no surprise since Costa Rica has been included in the empirical test (as distinct from Chile and Peru) on the assumption that latifundismo does not dominate the organization of productive activity in agriculture.[10]

Generally, it seems reasonable to conclude that although Costa Rica's structure of land tenure in combination with population increase appears to influence provincial net migration to some extent, it is not a dominant influence. Rather, a number of other influences emerge as important in the magnitudes and direction of Costa Rican provincial migration flows. In most cases, the direction of these influences is as hypothesized in the preceding chapter. It is also reasonable to argue that the findings for Costa Rica accord generally with the expectation of the theoretical model. That is, as the distribution of land to labor resources is considerably less uneven than in Chile and Peru, a large minifundio population is not expected to be subjected to extreme conditions of inadequate agricultural opportunities, nor is a labor, land, or credit market expected to be fully dependent on latifundistas. Accordingly, the incidence of net rural

10. In most of the remaining provinces, influences such as provincial urban-rural salary differentials, urban-rural unemployment differentials, and the level of rural literacy also appear to interact with the general conditions in agriculture to either stimulate or dampen the incidence of out-migration. For example, in the province of Puntarenas (17.8 percent of the sample population), with a rural net in-migration of 1.28, the stock and flow indexes of population pressure are low, the combined proportions of farms that are minifundios and land on latifundios are lowest (Figure 4.1a and b), the urban-rural salary differential is among the lowest (Figure 4.1e), the urban-rural unemployment differential is highest (Figure 4.1f), and the remaining urban-rural amenity differentials are low to moderate. The combined effect of all of these influences would suggest very little inducement to migrate out of the rural sector and apparently has acted to induce migrants to the area.

Again, in the provinces of Cartago (18.2 percent of the sample population) and Alajuela (30 percent of the sample population), the interaction of agricultural and nonagricultural influences is important. Thus, in the province of Cartago with a relatively high rate of out-migration of 3.10, the stock and flow indexes are highest, the combined proportion of population on minifundios and land held by latifundistas is among the highest, the urban-rural unemployment differential is among the lowest, and the remaining variables all assume moderate to low values. For the province of Alajuela, with a relatively low rate of migration of 0.53, the stock and flow indexes are moderate, the combined proportion of population on minifundios and proportion of land on latifundios is moderate, the urban-rural salary differential is among the highest but so too is the urban-rural unemployment differential, and the remaining variables take on a moderate to low value.

Finally, in the case of Heredia (8.5 percent of the sample population) with a migration rate of only 0.51, a moderate value for the stock and flow indexes and a high urban-rural salary differential is offset by the lowest urban-rural literacy differential and values for amenities which indicate that the rural sector is generally on a par with the urban sector. Again, then, we have the indication that our measures of population pressure and agricultural inopportunity do not adequately reflect conditions in the rural sector.

out-migration is not expected to be only a function of these kinds of conditions. Rather, as is observed, a range of additional factors is expected to exercise important pulls on potential rural migrants.

COLOMBIA

Evaluation of Colombian rural out-migration has been restricted on two counts: the small number of provinces for which basic measures could be estimated ($n = 12$) and limited access to data on variables other than the stock and flow indexes. Accordingly, analysis of the Colombian experience has been limited to the relationship between rates of total provincial rural population out-migration (not provincial rural male labor-force out-migration), and the stock and flow indexes.

Figure 4.2 graphs the provincial observations, weighted according to relative population size. Clearly, a relationship between the indexes of population pressure and agricultural inopportunity is evident. In fact, comparison of r^2 values for the stock and flow indexes (measured fully as for Chile and Costa Rica), and other more simple population pressure measures such as $P_t/(T_A - L_A)$ with $r^2 = 0.45$, or $P_t/$ (total nonsterile agricultural land) with $r^2 = 0.07$, reveals the same pattern as observed for Chile and Peru. At the very least, the conclusion seems reasonable that the experience of Colombia is in keeping with the theoretical model. As a policy consideration, it is also of some significance that the observations lying closest to the projected line represent the largest provincial populations.[11]

As further evidence in support of the model, we now turn briefly to a between-country analysis of Chile, Peru, Costa Rica, and Colombia, followed by an analysis of the migration experience of these countries in the broader context of Latin America as a whole.

11. In contrast to the approach and results reported here, the reader may wish to consult a recent study of Colombian migration in R. R. Nelson, T. P. Schultz, and R. L. Slighton (1971). The study, based largely on an earlier article by T. P. Schultz, identifies low rural wage levels and violence as important determinants of rural migration (overall R^2 was on the order of 0.3). Typically, however, the analysis fails to identify causes or mechanisms behind these factors. A statement that migration could be reduced if incomes were increased or if violence were reduced is largely empty. On the other hand, if low incomes and violence are linked to the minifundio-latifundio complex, then modification of the latter would seem not only relevant but possible.

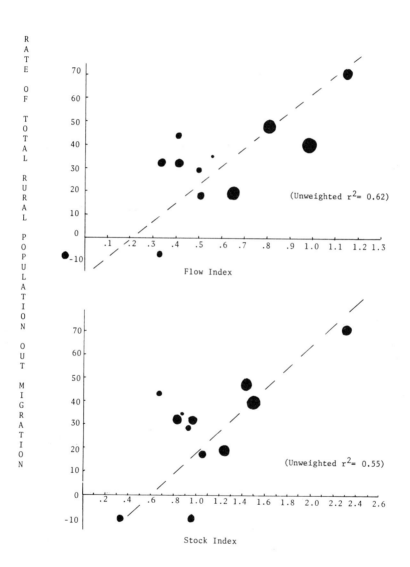

Figure 4.2. Stock and Flow Indexes and Migration in Colombia, 1951-64

It has already been pointed out that there are not only significant differences in the structure of land tenure and population growth within Chile, Peru, Costa Rica, and Colombia, but between them. In Chile, Peru, and Colombia, the distribution of labor to land resources has been described as extremely uneven and a host of qualitative studies testify to the various forms of agricultural inopportunity within the minifundio-latifundio complex. In contrast, the distribution of land to labor resources in Costa Rica has been described as considerably less uneven and both qualitative and statistical sources indicate that the minifundio-latifundio complex does not dominate the organization of productive activity to the same extent. Accordingly, if the theoretical model is an adequate description of the importance of variations in the system of land tenure and population growth as an influence in rural out-migration in Latin America, differences in these criteria between countries should be reflected in their magnitudes of rural out-migration.

In Table 4.11, differences in average yearly rates of rural population out-migration for the four countries appear to be highly related to differences in the structure of agriculture. For example, in Costa Rica, with one of the lowest rates of rural out-migration in Latin America and one of the most even distributions of labor to land resources, the average size of minifundios is almost twice that of Peruvian or Colombian minifundios and 2-1/2 times that of Chilean minifundios. Also, a large class of middle-sized farms holding 59 percent of the land in Costa Rica is available to provide employment for approximately 67.7 percent of the country's rural labor force in the landless employee class.[12] Turning to Peru, the structure of land tenure is approximately four times as uneven as that of Costa Rica, while the yearly rate of rural out-migration is nearly four times that of Costa Rica. As for the landless employee class in Peru, it is of considerably less importance. In the case of Chile, the distribution of land is somewhat less uneven than in Peru, yet the average size of minifundios is smaller and a very large landless employee class (70.2 percent) is reliant upon a small number of medium-sized farms holding only 16.7 percent of the country's agricultural land. In the

12. Although I do not assume that employment opportunities on latifundios are nonexistent, the data used for calculating the stock and flow indexes of population pressure indicate that for Peru and Costa Rica, latifundistas typically employ very small proportions of labor compared both to the land they hold and to the total landless employee class.

Table 4.11. Selected Demographic, Agricultural, and Economic Indicators for Chile, Peru, Costa Rica, and Colombia

Indicators	Chile 1952-60	Peru 1940-61	Costa Rica 1952-63	Colombia 1951-64
1. Average yearly rates of rural population out-migration	2.5	1.5	0.4	2.2
2. Proportion of farms (minifundios)	40.0	83.5	44.4[a] (28.8)	62.5
3. Average size of minifundios in hectares	1.1	1.5	2.7[a] (2.4)	1.6
4. Proportion of land on intermediate-sized farms	16.7	19.3	59.0	55.0
5. Proportion of land held by latifundios	80.0	75.0	32.4[a] (40.5)	40.5
6. Average size of latifundios in hectares	2,737.0	3,658.0	2,471.0[a] (1,460.0)	1,604.2
7. Approximate proportion of rural labor force in landless employee class	70.2	12.2	67.6	66.8
8. Proportion of country urban	64.0	41.4	34.4	45.8
9. Approximate urban-rural wage or salary differential[b]	2.84	1.76	1.33	2.60
10. Approximate urban-rural literacy differential[b]	1.40	2.08	1.23	1.44
11. National rate of population growth	2.2	1.6/3.0[c]	4.0	3.4

a. A minifundio in Costa Rica is a farm holding of less than 7 hectares; a latifundio, one larger than 700 hectares. The figures in parentheses are for minifundios defined as farm holdings less than 3.5 hectares and latifundios larger than 350 hectares.

b. The differentials here are all in favor of the urban area and, as such, are expressed as multiples of the rural values.

c. The two growth rates correspond to 1940-50 and 1950-61, respectively.

case of Colombia, high rates of population growth in combination with a large minifundio sector would appear to override the more favorable distribution of land to intermediate-sized farms.

We can also consider the effect of additional variables which are likely to be associated with conditions in agriculture. For example, the urban-rural wage or salary differential is low in Costa Rica and highest in Chile and Colombia. Chile is also considerably more urbanized than Colombia, Peru, and Costa Rica, with the implication that with both a positive urban-rural wage differential and a positive urban-rural literacy differential the obvious rural pushes may be reinforced by strong urban pulls. In fact, Chile has one of the highest rates of rural out-migration in Latin America over the 1950-60 period and is one of the few Latin American countries in which the absolute rural population declined over the decade.

As a final reflection on the relevance of the theoretical model for understanding rural migration in Latin America, consider the rural migration experience of sixteen Latin American economies in relation to the structure of their land-tenure systems (Table 4.12). Again, there is a strong indication of the significance of the distribution of land to labor resources as an important influence in rural out-migration. As Table 4.12 indicates, the average yearly rate of net rural out-migration for five countries with less than 50 percent of their farms minifundios and less than 50 percent of the land held by latifundistas is 0.56. In contrast, systematic increases in either the proportion of minifundios or the proportion of the land held by latifundistas are accompanied by a higher rate of out-migration. It is also interesting to find that as in the case of the provincial analyses for Chile, Peru, Costa Rica, and Colombia, rates of rural out-migration in the sixteen countries are higher when the proportion of land held by latifundistas is higher ($B = 1.96$) than when the proportion of farms that are minifundios is increased ($a_2b_2 = 1.80$). One possibility is that minifundio ownership implies ties to agriculture (possibly an inertia effect) whereas a large proportion of land held by latifundistas implies not only the host of uneconomical and exploitative conditions noted previously but possibly also greater awareness of relative deprivation among the rural poor, especially as their general level of education increases.

As a simple contrast to our approach to explaining rural migration in Latin America, a simple population density measure will be related to the measure of migration as in Table 4.13. It is clear, however, that considering only absolute population levels relative

Table 4.12. Average Yearly Rates of Rural Out-Migration for Sixteen Latin American Countries Classified by Proportion of Farms Less Than 5 Hectares and Proportion of Land on Farms Exceeding 500 Hectares[a]

	(A) Countries with 0-50% Land on Farms Exceeding 500 Hectares		(B) Countries with 50-100% Land on Farms Exceeding 500 Hectares	
	(a_1) 0-50% Farms <5 Hectares	(b_1) 50-100% Farms <5 Hectares	(b_1) 0-50% Farms <5 Hectares	(b_2) 50-100% Farms <5 Hectares
Rate of Rural Out-Migration	0.56 ($n = 5$)	1.48 ($n = 5$)	1.60 ($n = 3$)	2.33 ($n = 3$)

Sum rate for (A) = 1.02 ($n = 10$)

Sum rate for $a_1 b_1$ = 0.95 ($n = 8$)

Sum rate for (B) = 1.96 ($n = 6$)

Sum rate for $a_2 b_2$ = 1.80 ($n = 8$)

a. These rates have been calculated using national census data on the 1950-60 rural-urban distribution of the population, rates of natural increase compounded annually, etc. The agricultural data were obtained, for the most part, from the respective agricultural censuses of each country and, partly, from the series *The Statistical Abstract of Latin America* and *América en Cifras*. For each country, the rate of rural out-migration, proportion of farms less than 5 hectares in size, and proportion of land on farms greater than 500 hectares are given respectively: Costa Rica (0.4, 44.4, 38.0), Dominican Republic (0.8, 86.0, 30.0), El Salvador (1.4, 85.3, 23.8), Guatemala (0.9, 88.4, 40.0), Honduras (0.6, 49.0, 28.2), Mexico (2.3, 65.9, 83.0), Nicaragua (0.6, 42.0, 41.2), Panama (0.1, 45.8, 20.5), Argentina (2.2, 15.7, 75.0), Brazil (1.0, 44.8, 50.0), Colombia (1.6, 40.0, 80.0), Chile (2.8, 62.5, 40.5), Ecuador (1.5, 73.1, 45.0), Paraguay (2.3, 46.4, 28.0), Peru (1.6, 83.5, 75.0), and Venezuela (3.1, 51.0, 78.8).

to the land base without considering factors influencing the nature of productive activity utilizing labor and land is of little help in understanding the conditions leading to rural out-migration. Similar results were found when simple population density measures were included in the provincial analyses for Peru, Chile, Costa Rica, and Colombia.

TABLE 4.13. Yearly Rates of Net Rural Migration for 16 Latin American Countries Classified by Number of Rural Population per Square Kilometer of Arable Land, 1950-60

	Rural Population Density							
	0-49	50-99	100-149	150-99	200-249	250-99	300-349	350-99
Rate of Net Rural Out- Migration	-2.20 ($n=1$)	-1.90 ($n=2$)	-0.80 ($n=4$)	-1.65 ($n=2$)	-1.13 ($n=2$)	-0.80 ($n=3$)	-1.60 ($n=1$)	-1.85 ($n=1$)

DISCUSSION

The results of the empirical analyses indicate that an uneven distribution of labor to land resources in combination with relatively high rates of population growth is an important influence in Latin American rural migration. Possibly the strongest support for this explanation lies in findings for Chile and Peru where, of all factors considered, only those relating to the interaction of population growth and the uneven distribution of land to labor resources consistently accounted for a sizable proportion of the variation in the migration measure. Inasmuch as this study has been able to examine the impact of changes in the stocks and flows of labor demands within the minifundio-latifundio complex, there has been a systematic increase in the degree of association between refinements in these measures (first stocks, then flows, then both) and the migration measure. This indicates that population growth and the system of land tenure are at the basis of situations of economic stress and subsequently migration to areas offering seemingly greater opportunities.

It is also interesting to find that high proportions of land held by latifundistas are more significantly related to rates of out-migration than proportions of the rural population centralized on minifundios in both the within- and between-country analyses. This finding conforms to the theoretical model in that it implies that dominance of the rural-agricultural labor, land, and credit market by latifundistas affects the income-earning opportunities of not only those on minifundios but also the landless employee class. Finally, the fact that rural out-migration increases consistently and significantly with an increasing disparity in the distribution of labor to land in sixteen Latin American countries suggests that the model has theoretical relevance for explaining current patterns of rural population and labor-force redistribution in Latin America as a whole.

On the other hand, the reader may feel that the theoretical relevance of the model suffers due to the fact that the explanation given here is largely one-sided in its focus on population pressure, agricultural inopportunity, and possible situations of economic stress. As a means of evaluating this possibility, Costa Rica was deliberately included in the empirical analysis as a contrast to the experience of Chile, Peru, and Colombia. Also, a number of variables relating to urban-rural differentials were evaluated toward determining the influence of the "agricultural factor." Yet, in both the within- and between-country analyses, the results indicate that the more uneven the distribution of land to labor resources (holding constant or increasing population growth rates), the more this characteristic alone accounts for variations in the incidence of rural out-migration.

Concluding, it seems reasonable to propose that although it has not been possible to provide a rigorous test for the theoretical model, results of the empirical analysis are consistent with its implications. The next chapter addresses possibilities of influencing rural migration by manipulation of the structure of the land-tenure system.

5. Policy Considerations

IN THE preceding chapters, this study has been concerned with the occurrence of high rates of rural-urban migration in Latin America. It has attempted to explain variations in the incidence of rural out-migration largely in terms of situations of economic stress resulting from the interaction of increasing labor demands on the land and inequalities in the structure of the land-tenure system. By admission, the relevance of this explanation is limited to those economies with high rates of natural increase and a highly unequal distribution of labor to nonlabor resources. At the same time, as these influences are likely to exist in differing degrees (or may not exist at all in particular economies), we have suggested that the explanation should be useful as a classification scheme for differentiating the migration behavior of the countries of Latin America as a whole.

This chapter addresses pragmatic aspects of the inquiry—possibilities for controlling or influencing the pace of rural-urban population redistribution in Latin America. This issue is important in the sense that a more balanced, optimal redistribution of the rural-urban population in many Latin American countries may require curtailment of current rural-urban migratory flows.[1] On the basis of government perceptions of migration and urbanization problems (see Chapter 1), it is certainly reasonable to proceed as if

1. That a rural-urban drift is likely to be inevitable over the long run is not the issue here; it is the desirability of the pace and direction of the present drift that is of concern.

rural-urban population distribution has become overbalanced on the urban side (that is, more urbanized than industrialized or developed in other respects) and as if current migration flows are excessive.

Clearly, the ability to influence migration rests on the degree to which its occurrence can be accounted for by the mechanisms of "explanation" and "prediction." Further, if the vehicle for control is to be national policy or planning, then knowledge will be required of (1) the causal forces which operate to stimulate or curtail rural out-migration in specific Latin American countries, (2) the effect of eliminating these causal forces or reducing their presence, and (3) the feasibility of programs for effecting change in the causal forces.

The first issue has already been addressed, i.e., major influences which operate to stimulate a rural exodus in select Latin American countries. These consist of (1) the interaction of increasing population and labor demands on the land and (2) inequalities in the structure of the land-tenure system. Accordingly, to curtail the rural exodus in Latin American countries which meet our initial criteria, it follows that one or both of these influences require modification. For the balance of this study emphasis will be placed on possible effects of modifying the land-tenure system; modification of rates of natural increase will not be considered for three reasons:

1. While a decline in the rate of natural increase would probably ease economic stress for some, and might even result in lower rates of rural out-migration, improvements in rural-agricultural standards of living for the majority of the population would probably be minimal. That is, if the description of the nature of productive activity given in this study is accurate, moderating population increase without moderating the distribution of income-earning opportunities would merely serve to maintain the status quo. Indeed, some researchers claim that positive economic effects can be attributed to population growth (and population pressure), such as demands for new forms of labor-intensive technology, new inputs, and the challenging of institutional forms which may be impeding efficient resource use (E. Boserup 1967, A. O. Hirschman 1958).

Now, let there be no misunderstanding. This study does not maintain that increased population growth and pressure, accompanied by the threat of starvation and high child mortality rates, are useful as fuel for accelerating revolution (i.e., violent agrarian reform). Our point is merely that "population pressure" in rural Latin America is more likely to be a problem of failure to increase living standards through utilization of actual and potentially productive resources available to a growing population than one of population growth per se. Of course, if a true saturation of rural-agricultural income-generating possibilities for the rural-agricultural population actually existed, then fertility reduction would take on singular importance. Our analysis, however, suggests that this is not the case in many economies of Latin America.

2. There is little certainty as to how a decline in the rate of natural increase can best be brought about. Rates of natural increase in Latin America increased steadily over the 1940-61 period due largely to effective mortality control through improved health and sanitary measures. Needless to say, abandonment of these types of programs as a means of reducing natural increase would meet serious ethical challenges. On the other hand, reducing natural increase involves many more hurdles than simply meeting the costs of family planning services. Motivating the population as a whole to use family planning services and diffusing information are the major problems. This is particularly so in rural-agricultural areas where infant mortality rates and illiteracy are high—conditions which generally run counter to acceptance of family planning services. A key implication of the economic theory of fertility is that married couples are likely to curtail their own reproductive behavior (by means of contraceptive techniques already available) once their economic situation begins to improve and they envision high opportunity costs to be forgone with additional numbers of children (R. A. Easterlin 1969). The author's position (R. P. Shaw 1974c) is that, over the long run, improvements in agricultural income-earning possibilities as a first and foremost planning objective will be accompanied by a reduction in the prevalence of conditions and attitudes that typically are associated with high fertility. Of course, over the short run, higher standards of living are also apt to result in greater reproductive potential due to less risk of miscarriage, better nutrition of females, and declining rates of widowhood. It is also probable that the response to a disequilibrium between actual and expected or desired family size due to declining infant mortality rates (i.e., a standard-of-living and health-related factor) will be lagged, as individual households are not likely to perceive immediately the impact of declining infant mortality rates on family size. The key consideration here, however, is that an excess of actual family size over its expected or desired size (and the implications of a too-large family in pursuing a higher standard of living) should produce the

sustained motivation necessary for an individual household to curtail its own fertility.

3. Formulation and implementation of policies designed to curtail reproductive behavior will meet much fiercer opposition than those designed to stimulate land redistribution. Almost all governments of Latin America have land reform laws on the books; the same does not apply for population policies (particularly fertility control policies). For example, the Peruvian government rejects birth control as a "palliative" measure which leads to neglect of "required structural changes fundamental to socioeconomic development." While Colombia tends toward the Peruvian position and Chile and Costa Rica endorse birth control, the view that development is a prerequisite to motivation to use birth control is widely held. In fact, during the recent World Population Conference, a strong consensus emerged that a major weakness of the "Draft World Population Plan of Action" was its failure to emphasize development first. A notable reversal of a typically Western point of view was made by J. D. Rockefeller III (president of the Population Council of New York) that emphasis on reducing population growth without development is not likely to have tangible results. Of course, this view marries well with the economic theory of fertility and the notion that couples should have the right to both decide on and attain their desired family size. Should the number of children conceived and surviving come to exceed the number expected and desired, then family limitation methods should be made available as a basic human welfare measure. Expressing population growth in this way obviously shifts emphasis to those factors which "condition" desired and expected family size (see R. P. Shaw 1974c).

MODIFYING THE LAND-TENURE SYSTEM

In addressing this issue, we are actually concerned with whether changes in the organization of productive activity within the minifundio-latifundio complex will serve to curtail the flow of rural out-migrants. That is, as this study has argued that high rates of rural out-migration are positively associated with a poverty of agricultural opportunities or income-producing possibilities near subsistence levels, it is now concerned with evaluating possible means of reducing the poverty of agricultural opportunities and increasing rural-agricultural income-earning possibilities.

Modification of the structure of land tenure represents only one type of change (though an important one) and it is important to bear in mind that changes in availability of regional and local credit, markets for the distribution of produce, etc., also constitute important changes in the nature of productive activity in Latin American agriculture. At the same time, it is important to guard against considering policy or planning possibilities that are not warranted on the basis of the research findings. For this reason, focus is primarily on an evaluation of the possible improvement of agricultural incomes and resulting reduced rates of rural out-migration when the structure of land tenure is modified. Emphasis is on empirical studies as against theoretical arguments. Generally, theoreticians attribute positive effects to land redistribution such as (1) contributions in the form of rises in output and productivity, (2) factor contributions in the form of additions to the available supply of inputs, (3) market contributions in the form of an increasing role of agriculture and its population as a market for the consumption and investment goods of other sectors of the economy, (4) improved welfare and living standards due to increased productivity and increased distributive equity, and (5) increased participation in civic affairs and self-government.

Clues from Aggregative Data on the Four Sample Countries.—As a first indication of the impact of modifying the structure of land tenure on rates of rural out-migration in Latin America, we need only draw on the implications of the cross-sectional analysis in Chapter 4. In Chile, Peru, Costa Rica, and Colombia, the regression and graphic analyses suggest that reducing the proportion of farms that are minifundios will be moderately associated with lower rates of rural out-migration, whereas a reduction in the proportion of land held by latifundistas will be highly associated with lower rates of rural out-migration. Of course, this kind of inference is not drawn on the basis of results of the cross-sectional analysis per se. It is only within the context of the theoretical model, and the entire set of bottlenecks discussed, that causation and operational policy guidelines are implied.

In terms of a redistribution of land to more families, insights into potential improvements in agricultural income-producing possibilities are available from aggregate data on land use by farm size. In Table 5.1, land use data for Chile, Peru, Costa Rica, and Colombia suggest that land is used much more intensively on minifundios than

Table 5.1. Land Use Data by Farm Size--Chile, Peru, Costa Rica, and Colombia[a]

	Farms	

Chile (1955)

	<5 Hectares	>500 Hectares
Number of farms	55,961	6,449
% of total farms	37.0	4.0
Number of hectares	78,116	22,397,330
% of total agricultural land	0.2	80.8
Land use		
% of land cultivated	73.6	12.6
% yield crops	52.1	5.7
% other	21.5	6.9
% of land uncultivated	12.6	62.5
% wooded area	2.1	15.3
% pastures	10.3	47.1
% sterile land	13.8	24.9

Peru (1961)

	<5 Hectares	>5 Hectares
Number of farms	726,132	143,813
% of total farms	83.4	16.6
Number of hectares	1,036,188	16,685,857
% of total agricultural land	6.1	93.9
Land use		
% of land cultivated	80.1	16.9
% yield crops	60.0	5.8
% other	20.2	11.1
% permanent cultivation	6.0	1.9
% natural pastures	9.3	50.6
% wooded area	1.7	11.8
% unproductive land	3.0	18.8

Costa Rica (1955)

	<3.5 Hectares	>350 Hectares
Number of farms	2,758	561
% of total farms	6.7	3.4
Number of hectares	33,400	1,125,249
% of total agricultural land	1.3	43.8
Land use		
% of land cultivated	43.0	5.0
% yield crops	39.5	0.8
% idle land	3.0	4.1
% other	2.5	0.1
% permanently cultivated land	37.0	6.0
% permanent pastures	14.0	40.0
% wooded area	4.0	49.0

Colombia (1960)

	<5 Hectares	>500 Hectares
Number of farms	756,605	6,902
% of total farms	62.5	0.6
Number of hectares	1,239,000	11,052,000
% of total agricultural land	4.5	40.5
Land use		
% of land cultivated	46.7	3.9
% yield crops	35.9	1.3
% other	10.8	2.5
% permanent cultivation	23.9	0.8
% natural pastures	17.7	69.7
% wooded area	3.8	21.6
% all other	7.9	4.1

a. Source: Respective national agricultural censuses.

on latifundios.[2] This may come as no surprise, however, given that 37 percent of Chile's farms, 83.4 percent of Peru's farms, and 62.5 percent of Colombia's farms have only 0.2 percent, 6.1 percent, and 4.5 percent of the total agricultural land, respectively. The situation in Costa Rica is, of course, much less acute since land is more equally distributed. The land use data for farms which are minifundios and latifundios, however, are comparable with those for Chile and Peru.

Another indication that minifundios are more productive in their land use than latifundios is provided in Table 5.2; the data were prepared by the Inter-American Committee for Agricultural Development in its studies of land tenure in seven Latin American countries (CIDA 1966). In this table, subfamily farms and multifamily large farms are generally representative of minifundios and latifundios respectively. Clearly, given the data for the average value of production per agricultural and cultivated hectare for the two farm groups, a redistribution of agricultural and cultivated land to the smaller-sized farms would suggest major increases in output per unit of land. Of course, an important question here is whether latifundio land could actually be redistributed for intensive cultivation.

Data for Peru and Colombia (Tables 5.3 and 5.4) relate to the above question. Of principal interest in Table 5.3 is the fact that in almost every Peruvian province, the number of hectares of land cultivable but not worked (i.e., idle land) exceeds the total number of cultivable hectares available to minifundios. In many provinces, the number of cultivable hectares not worked on latifundios exceeds the total agricultural land available to minifundio farms. Redistribution of land in both countries would certainly suggest increased income-earning prospects for the minifundio and landless employee class. It must be mentioned, however, that the determination of whether idle land was arable was made by the owner or the person who filled out the census form. A safe position would be that some capital investment may be required to bring this land into production (i.e., to drain, clear, irrigate, level, fence, buy livestock or machinery, or fertilize).

2. For Peru, land use data are available only for farms classified as smaller than 5 hectares or larger than 5 hectares. However, as a relatively small proportion of the country's total farms are between 5 and 500 hectares (19 percent), we may refer to farms larger than 5 hectares as latifundios without fear of significant distortion. For Costa Rica, under 3.5 hectares and over 350 hectares define minifundios and latifundios, respectively.

Table 5.2. Value of Agricultural Production by Size of Farm Groups--Chile (1955)[a]

| | Farm Classifications[b] | | | | |
	Subfamily	Family	Multifamily Medium	Multifamily Large	Sum
1. % of total in each country					
Agricultural land	0[c]	8	13	79	100
Agricultural workers	13	28	21	38	100
Value of production	4	16	23	57	100
2. Agricultural production					
Total value (000s of escudos)	22,500	81,097	117,112	299,816	
Value per exploitation	404	1,343	4,794	28,876	
3. Average value of production (escudos)					
Per agricultural hectare	334	46	41	41	
Per cultivable hectare	391	126	96	83	
Per worker	268	443	828	1,171	

a. Source: S. Barraclough and A. L. Domike (1966).

b. Subfamily farms are defined as farms large enough to provide employment for less than two people with the typical incomes, markets, and levels of technology and capital now prevailing in each region; family farms are defined as farms large enough to provide employment for 2 to 3.9 people on the assumption that most of the farm work is being carried out by the members of the farm family; multifamily medium farms consist of 4 to 12 people; and multifamily large farms contain more than 12 people.

Table 5.3. Hectares of Land Used for Cultivation on Minifundios and Hectares of Cultivable Land Not Worked on Latifundios--Peru and Colombia

Province	Minifundios			Farms >500 Hectares with Cultivable Land Not Worked	
	% of Total Farms <5 Hectares	Number of Farms <5 Hectares	Total Hectares Cultivable	% of Total Farms	Hectares Cultivable but Not Worked
Peru[a]					
Tumbes	92.4	2,930	1,730	2.1	560
Piura	90.0	34,695	30,191	2.8	25,278
Cajamarca	79.9	87,302	108,113	8.7	88,671
La Libertad	78.4	27,533	39,628	8.6	173,097
Ancash	89.3	68,348	80,203	4.9	58,689
Huánuco	77.3	37,324	44,520	13.3	52,899
Junín	88.8	49,460	47,839	4.0	56,218
Lima	84.2	31,580	28,399	6.3	42,122
Ica	73.0	5,450	4,874	7.6	13,494
Huancavelica	91.1	47,447	58,672	6.6	38,954
Ayacucho	88.0	57,648	67,982	5.9	31,003
Cuzco	88.0	57,535	53,596	5.6	142,060
Apurímac	93.0	38,656	34,892	3.0	40,975
Puno	83.6	96,332	57,440	7.9	175,285
Moquegua	93.0	6,227	6,011	2.2	667
Tacna	75.1	3,591	5,147	8.0	5,354
Loreto	82.2	18,458	16,001	6.3	43,033
San Martín	31.2	3,855	3,812	30.4	32,864
Lambayeque	76.0	9,970	11,279	7.6	18,374

Colombia[b]

Antioquia	70.5	119,356	109,621	0.4	36,427
Atlántico	66.5	7,914	8,737	0.6	2,379
Bolívar	62.5	39,885	40,627	1.0	20,050
Boyacá	68.2	131,236	138,067	0.6	9,172
Cauca	63.1	46,529	60,120	0.3	7,981
Cundinamarca	69.4	100,623	113,037	0.2	11,197
Huila	47.0	16,308	20,359	0.7	5,928
Magdalena	54.4	29,949	29,216	2.2	71,581
Nariño	67.3	60,733	77,139	0.1	5,478
Notre de Santander	38.5	15,050	23,096	0.4	6,696
Santander	51.3	46,126	60,507	0.5	33,154
Tolima	51.9	37,460	49,887	0.6	29,313

a. Source: 1961 Census of Agriculture, Peru.

b. Source: 1960 Census of Agriculture, Colombia.

Table 5.4. Provincial Land Use Data--Chile, Peru, and Colombia

Province	% of Farm Land Used for Cultivation		% of Provincial Agricultural Land Used for Cultivation	% of Provincial Agricultural Land on Latifundios
	Minifundios[b]	Latifundios[b]		
Chile (1955)				
Aconcagua	96.3	9.9	12.5	93.9
Valparaíso	79.2	23.6	25.6	84.3
Santiago	70.7	16.6	24.1	87.0
O'Higgins	87.6	25.4	39.0	73.6
Colchagua	86.9	3.7	40.0	79.6
Curicó	84.2	18.4	30.0	73.2
Talca	93.8	2.2	40.5	76.8
Maule	71.0	27.5	34.1	62.1
Linares	89.0	39.4	47.6	66.6
Ñuble	88.5	35.1	49.8	61.7
Bío-Bío	81.7	34.2	41.2	73.9
Malleco	88.2	32.3	42.3	70.7
Cautín	86.6	54.7	61.0	39.3
Osorno	86.4	34.9	45.6	68.0
Llanquihue	71.5	14.1	26.0	58.7
Peru (1940-61)				
Tumbes	50.0	3.8	11.8	88.0
Piura	62.0	13.3	26.3	82.2
Cajamarca	70.0	14.7	31.8	59.2
La Libertad	78.0	14.2	32.7	84.4
Ancash	75.5	13.3	26.8	74.3
Huánuco	67.0	7.9	24.3	63.0

Junín	85.3	4.8	16.1	76.5
Lima	70.0	14.0	22.5	75.3
Ica	74.3	57.0	70.6	49.0
Huancavelica	79.8	9.5	23.0	68.8
Ayacucho	80.0	15.7	28.7	56.3
Cuzco	71.5	5.6	18.1	81.1
Apurímac	87.2	4.8	19.7	82.3
Puno	51.5	2.7	10.3	80.0
Moquegua	80.0	10.4	14.6	90.0
Tacna	77.7	8.5	17.3	70.0
Loreto	49.8	9.0	57.0	66.7
San Martín	44.2	26.8	60.0	9.2
Lambayeque	75.3	35.0	43.8	82.6
Colombia				
Antioquia	66.0	2.8	19.8	28.8
Atlántico	69.2	2.0	12.6	21.0
Bolívar	59.2	1.1	11.1	37.1
Boyacá	45.5	4.5	11.2	62.0
Cauca	64.3	3.9	25.4	23.3
Cundinamarca	50.4	5.6	31.4	18.5
Huila	64.0	2.2	15.8	29.8
Magdalena	70.4	2.5	12.4	49.7
Nariño	63.7	4.3	43.1	8.2
Notre de Santander	63.0	2.9	30.0	17.7
Santander	52.9	3.3	26.5	24.2
Tolima	72.6	4.1	27.0	27.3

a. Source: Respective national censuses of agriculture.

b. For both Chile and Peru, a minifundio represents a farm holding of less than 5 hectares. For Chile, a latifundio is a farm holding in excess of 500 hectares, and for Peru, due to data limitations, a farm holding in excess of 5 hectares (all farms 5-500 hectares in Peru constitute only 19 percent of the total farms).

In Table 5.4, land use data are again provided for Chile and Peru. In this case, however, the data are for proportions of land used for cultivation at the provincial level. Of principal interest here is the association between the proportion of provincial agricultural land used for cultivation and the proportion of provincial land on latifundios. In the case of Chile, the simple linear regression correlation coefficient is −0.74 (−0.85 for a weighted analysis); for Peru the coefficient is −0.59 (−0.70 for a weighted analysis), and for Colombia, −0.79. In other words, the more provincial land that is held by latifundistas, the less that is cultivated. If we knew nothing of the nature of productive activity within the minifundio-latifundio complex, we might argue that the proportion of provincial land used for cultivation approximates the actual cultivable land and that where this proportion is small, latifundios or large-scale farms with labor-extensive technology proliferate to the advantage of the economy. A more realistic interpretation, however, is that where latifundismo is of less predominance, the majority of the rural-agricultural population is successful in preparing the land for cultivation. In this sense, it is likely that land use data—especially land use data for latifundios—are misleading as to the uses to which land might be put. That is, the potential for land use (and especially cultivation of land) may never be realized until the highly productive minifundio/landless worker is able to apply his traditional labor-intensive methods to presently withheld land.

As a further indication that rural-agricultural income-producing possibilities might be extended through land redistribution, an average farm size has been calculated for Chile (1955), Peru (1961), and Colombia (1960), shown in Table 5.5. The calculations were made by dividing total provincial nonsterile agricultural land by an estimate of the total number of provincial rural-agricultural families. The table refers only to an equal distribution of land, not to optimal farm size with respect to the type of land and nonland inputs available. That is, given the host of additional factors which would be likely to influence returns to labor on the land, this type of calculation tells us little about the likelihood of increasing levels of living should an extensive land redistribution be introduced. The calculations in Table 5.5 do, however, suggest that potential for improvement in the agricultural situation in these countries is immense, especially considering that the average farm size of 37 percent of Chile's farm-operator families and 83.4 percent of Peru's farm-operator families approximates a meager 1.4 hectares.

Table 5.5. Calculated "Best Average Farm Size"--Provinces of Chile, Peru, and Colombia

Chile (1960)	Best Average Farm Size in Hectares	Peru (1961)	Best Average Farm Size in Hectares	Colombia (1960)	Best Average Farm Size in Hectares
Aconcagua	67.0	Tumbes	17.6	Antioquía	16.3
Valparaíso	36.6	Piura	12.7	Atlántico	23.2
Santiago	37.2	Cajamarca	10.1	Bolívar	28.6
O'Higgins	19.0	La Libertad	20.1	Boyacá	22.2
Colchagua	37.3	Ancash	14.4	Cauca	13.0
Curicó	36.2	Huánuco	16.0	Cundinamarca	10.5
Talca	36.0	Junín	25.0	Huila	28.8
Maule	57.5	Lima	19.3	Magdalena	59.1
Linares	32.5	Ica	9.0	Nariño	7.7
Ñuble	43.0	Huancavelica	15.2	Notre de Santander	21.3
Bío-Bío	50.3	Ayacucho	18.0	Santander	20.3
Malleco	77.0	Cuzco	24.3	Tolima	22.7
Cautín	36.7	Apurímac	14.0		
Osorno	60.3	Puno	30.5		
Llanquihue	62.4	Moquegua	32.0		
		Tacna	38.3		
		Loreto	11.7		
		San Martín	13.0		
		Lambayeque	21.4		

a. Source: Calculated using data from respective national censuses of agriculture and population.

A more conclusive way of evaluating the effects of modifying the land-tenure system of migration would be to estimate changes in the stock and flow indexes over time compared to changes in rates of provincial rural out-migration. Unfortunately, only in the case of Chile has it been possible to compare variations in migration and the stock and flow indexes between time t and $t + n$. Even so, there are two major data problems limiting the evaluation: (1) the 1970 census of population data is not available for each province (i.e., provincial figures have been grouped), thus time-series comparisons are limited to a few provinces; and (2) since Chile's Census of Agriculture was enumerated in 1965, only partial effects of Chile's rigorous agrarian reform program are reflected in census statistics. Nevertheless, it is reassuring to find that the largest drops in rates of rural out-migration are recorded for the provinces of Aconcagua and O'Higgins, where there have been (1) a reduction in the average size of latifundios from 9,573 hectares to 3,265 hectares, and from 1,867 hectares to 967 hectares, respectively; (2) a reduction in proportion of total land on latifundios of 6.1 percent and 20.5 percent, respectively; and (3) a decline in the stock index of population pressure and agricultural inopportunity of 58 percent and 30 percent, respectively. Conversely, for the provinces of Curicó, Talca, and Linares (combined), out-migration increased along with an increase in the stock index and proportion of minifundio farms.

In the case of Costa Rica, 1973 Census of Agriculture data are presently available but, unfortunately, farm size classifications are not continuous in the 1973 published tables. Even so, distribution of land between minifundios and latifundios does not appear to have changed much and fractionalization of minifundios seems to have enlarged this farm subgroup.

Clues from the Literature.—Conclusions which can be drawn from the empirical data above are at best impressionistic. It is not yet possible to assert that land redistribution will result in higher income-earning possibilities. Nor is it possible to conclude that increased income-producing possibilities resulting from land redistribution will operate to curtail rural out-migration. To address the former issue, it has been necessary to turn to literature on Latin America in general and studies of the effects of land redistribution on productivity.[3] Although many studies have been conducted in

3. Inefficiencies in resource use among latifundios and inadequate land for the minifundio and landless employee class have already been discussed in Chapter 2. In this section, we are more concerned with the actual effects of redistributing these resources.

isolation from one another, or pertain to the preliminary results of short-duration land reform programs or trial programs at the local or community level, cumulatively they provide a great deal more information than has previously been available. In many respects they suggest that the rationale and policy behind land reform is well directed.

As an overview, P. Dorner, M. Brown, and D. Kanel (1969) observe: "It might be argued that the higher productivity per unit of land on existing small farms is no real evidence that new units to be created by splitting up large farms would increase productivity. But the evidence available on post reform in Mexico, Bolivia, Chile, Japan, Taiwan, Egypt, Yugoslavia, demonstrates that average productivity per unit land increased rather substantially after the reforms—reforms which in all cases involved a reduction in size of farm units." D. Warriner (1973) concludes, on the basis of extensive experience in land reform, "past and present, land reform can be expected to do at least one very important thing: to raise peasant living standards by raising peasant incomes. At lower levels of living, in the world's dietary deficiency regions where the income elasticity of demand for food is high, most of this increase will be consumed in food." She also notes that "because land-use potential is much greater in these Latin American systems than it is in Asia, the expectation of a major contribution to development through reform is also greater."

One of the soundest theoretical and empirical studies of the benefits to be had from redistributing land from latifundios to minifundios has been undertaken by W. R. Cline (1970). In Cline's study of the economic consequences of land reform in Brazil, he concludes that land redistribution causes increased productivity because of two empirical relationships—constant returns to scale coupled with greater intensity of land use on smaller farms. Of particular interest are Cline's calculation of scale economies and his test of the hypothesis that land is used more intensively on small farms, with this intensity not accounted for by land quality. In calculating scale economies, Cline distinguishes efficiencies in terms of only those resources actually employed on the farm as against all available resources. Large farms using only a small proportion of their land are likely to operate under decreasing returns. By assembling data on eighteen product sectors representing about one-third of Brazil's total production and by employing statistical tests (i.e., estimation of a Cobb-Douglas production function), Cline finds decreasing returns to scale for 90 percent of his sample.

In testing for intensity of land use, Cline regresses farm areas against proportions of productive farm area, value added per farm, and inputs of land cultivated, labor, seed, fertilizer, and capital. Proportion of productive farm area is related negatively to farm size in 90 percent of the sample and almost all factors of production are applied less intensively as farm size increases.

In evaluating agricultural productivity resulting from land redistribution, Cline simulates two types of reform for each product sector in turn. One is based on a total reform that redistributes all land evenly. The other constitutes a partial reform that affects only farms with over 300 hectares. Built into the simulations are assumptions of both high and low levels of unemployment and change and no change in levels of seed, fertilizer, and capital.

The effect of the total reform is positive and substantial in 85 percent of the product sectors, with the partial reform less successful but substantial for 30 percent of the product sectors and only one sector showing reductions in production. These results hold generally with variations in the assumptions and conditions. Cline concludes that if land redistribution is undertaken for reasons of social equity alone, the production results will not be injurious to the economy. Rather, as his model predicts, the results will be largely positive with an overall increase in output of about 20 percent.

In a study of changes in agricultural production in Mexico from 1940 to 1965, R. Hertford (1969) examines the performance of the "ejido" — a farm unit of approximately 19 hectares of redistributed farm land.[4] Hertford points out that up to 1965, some 45 million hectares of agricultural land were expropriated by the Mexican government, and by 1940, ejidos held some 29 percent of Mexico's arable land, 43 percent of its cropland, 50 percent of its publicly irrigated land, and 54 percent of all farms, producing 41 percent of the value of gross crop production. By Hertford's calculations (based on multiple-regression techniques), the long-run performance of the ejido sector has been good in the sense that output to cropland harvested was about as good for the ejido sector as for the private sector over the 1940-62 period. Hertford concludes that from a social equity position, Mexico's land redistribution policies have been beneficial, total agricultural output has increased, and the ejido sector has performed as a better output maximizer than the private sector.

---

4. An ejido is a land-tenure arrangement by which land is granted to a group of farmers to be cultivated either individually or collectively. The land unit must be cultivated at least every other year.

Hertford's conclusions receive general support in studies by D. E. Horton (1968) and F. Dovring (1970b). Dovring argues that Mexican land reform has "in no way been at the expense of economic progress" and that land reform has steered more of the nation's resources into labor-intensive growth in agriculture. In a 1969 study, J. W. Mellor finds that between 1940 and 1950, the performance of the Mexican land reform sector fell behind the private sector, but from 1950 to 1960 it surpassed the private sector. In a study of three ejidos in Jalisco, Mexico, N. C. Clement (1968) argues that the ejido is an efficient way of absorbing labor surplus and that it is making a contribution to high rates of agricultural output per land area. Finally, D. Warriner (1973) claims that Mexico is "the great success story from the raw beginnings which over 50 years ago led to the biggest reform in the world; after 1950 to the highest rate of growth of agricultural productivity in the world."

Bolivia is another Latin American country in which land reform has been under way for some time. Generally, positive effects have been attributed to the program. For example, in a study of production on four Bolivian ex-haciendas (i.e., ex-latifundios), M. Burke (1968) evaluates the impact of land reform by comparing output with that of four Peruvian haciendas. As expected, he finds output per worker higher on the Peruvian haciendas but output per land area higher on the Bolivian ex-haciendas. He also attributes positive effects to the land reform in terms of increasing incomes and higher levels of education and literacy for Indian workers, a considerably less unequal distribution of incomes, and greater integration of the majority of the self-employed farmers into the market. M. Peinado (1969) finds essentially the same thing in his study of the dissolution of two Bolivian haciendas after the 1953 reform. Size of land holding, market participation, incomes, unionized control of resources, availability of education, and access to political involvement all increased considerably. One of the haciendas (the one with the best land) sells roughly seven times more of its produce than before reform; overall per capita incomes have reached levels 60 percent higher than the national average.

R. J. Clark's (1968) study of land reform in the northern highlands of Bolivia also reveals that peasants now participate in and benefit from cash markets whereas in the previous system of land tenure the production, transportation, and marketing of goods was largely an unremunerated obligation of the peasant. In contrast to an erroneous report by FAO that production declined after reform, Clark shows what really happened: much of the output was marketed through different channels after reform. The FAO observer, in his monitoring of output for marketing, did not discover this fact for several years. C. Camacho-Saa (1967) found that labor surplus was considerably less on larger Bolivian minifundios than on the microminifundios, and in a study by U. Reye (1967), increased civil rights and education for Indian workers and increases in agricultural productivity of up to 35 percent between 1956 and 1962 were attributed to Bolivian land redistribution programs.

Instances of unsuccessful Bolivian reform have been noted primarily in the southeastern highlands. The reason, as given by D. Heyduk (1973), is that only a semblance of land redistribution has taken place (resulting from loss of title by absentee owners); actual redistribution of land among new families has not taken place. Before "title transfer," almost all latifundista land was in use in a tenant system. However, tenant parcels were of highly unequal size, a tenant class system existed, and tenants of large parcels farmed sections out to subtenants. Title transfer meant only that large and small tenants received title to the parcels they had been operating all along. In Heyduk's words (1973, p. 92),

> At many ex-haciendas therefore, the agrarian reform solidified and reinforced the peasant hierarchy, making peasant hacendados (relatively large holdings) more secure and maintaining the insecurity of subtenants and landless dependents. . . . The proportion of land to actually change hands as a result of the agrarian reform was fairly small. . . . for those who worked the land and who made up the great majority of the population, the results were for the most part inconsequential.

In many of the remaining countries of Latin America, land reform programs have just been getting under way since their congressional sanction in the late 1950s or early 1960s. In the case of Peru, one study attributes positive effects to a local land redistribution program (A. R. Holmberg and H. F. Dobyns 1969), although the consensus seems to be that land redistribution has been slow and ineffective (E. Flores 1970, V. I. Leonova 1970). On the basis of an analysis of four ex-haciendas in Peru, D. E. Horton (1972) argues that a basic failing has been the shift from haciendas to large technical cooperatives. In other terms, agrarian reform has failed to contain the basic principles of (1) increased rural employment and (2) reduction of poverty through redistribution of incomes, i.e., transfer of property titles to more operator households. The Peruvian government began by first expropriating the wealthy sugar plantations along the coast, then the ranches along the Andes. For example, land was seized from the U.S.-tied Cerro corporation 80 miles east of Huancayo and given over to about 400 ranch hands and 3,000 families in 16 Indian communities. However, the transition to a large technical cooperative has been received as if it were a simple change of management, mainly because the bulk of the profits go to repay the government for the property's mortgage, reinvestment in livestock, and roads.

In Chile, land redistribution, which started with the Alessandri administration in the 1950s, has been described by W. C. Thiesenhusen (1966, 1970) as successful with respect to increasing output and prospects for employment. However, as revealed by K. Esser (1970), Frei's agrarian reform program was not effective in expropriating the property of the 4.2 percent of the landholders who controlled 80.9 percent of the agricultural land and water rights, because they were protected by the constitution. Nor did the program tackle problems associated with prohibited agricultural trade unions (up to 1966-68) or the fact that rural-agricultural illiterates were not allowed to vote. J. Ziche (1971) reports that between 1965 and July 1970, some 1,319 large estates holding 280,000 hectares of irrigated land and 3 million hectares of dry land were expropriated and redistributed to some 30,000 families in 910 collectivities, but again this represents only about 10 percent of the claimable land in the hands of large landholders. C. Barriaga (1972) further reports that in Allende's first six months in office 700 farms with approximately 1,760,000 hectares were expropriated and by March 1972, another 2,000 farms had also been expropriated, leaving only about 1,000 to 1,200 latifundio farms remaining in the entire country.

Colombian reform has placed solid emphasis on clarifying and issuing land titles. Over the last decade, title transfer has been slow and costly, meaning that legal transfers have not always been recorded. As land ownership is crucial to control, credit, and sociopolitical representation in the community, land titles play an important role in the security of the small landholder. During its first five years, the Colombian Institute of Agrarian Reform granted land titles covering 1,784,000 hectares (15.8 percent of total latifundio land) to 47,000 families who worked the land themselves (about 5 percent of the agricultural population). While redistribution has obviously been slow, D. W. Adams and L. E. Montero (1965) provide yet another example of positive benefits from the parcelization of 1,500 acres in Colombia's tobacco region, in the form of 850 people maintaining "a very satisfactory living" as against a previous 70 on the hacienda.

Generally, the studies above support the proposition that reforms which redistribute land from latifundistas to the majority of the rural-agricultural population lead to increases in rural-agricultural levels of living if not increases in agricultural production. On a more conservative note we might side with D. W. Adams' (1973) statement that most "country reviews" support the conclusion that land reform has a neutral to positive impact on production. At the very least, it can be argued that there will be a higher total factor productivity when land is redistributed to small farmholders because the present labor surplus results in a high social cost of labor.

Whether such programs would curtail rural-agricultural out-migration, however, is infinitely more difficult to ascertain. To the author's knowledge, this issue has not been addressed empirically in the literature to date. Accordingly, the only answer to this question can be that it would seem, then, on the basis of (1) the literature reviewed, (2) the implications of the theoretical model, and (3) the cross-sectional results for Chile, Peru, Costa Rica, Colombia, and Latin America as a whole, that greater equality in the distribution of rural land and incomes would probably cause at least some relaxation of the forces currently stimulating high rates of rural out-migration. It is also realistic to recognize that while land reform may not be a cure-all, it is the only alternative presently available for making inroads on rural income inequality and minifundio poverty.

A NOTE ON EFFECTING LAND REDISTRIBUTION PROGRAMS

As T. Lynn Smith (1957, 1965, 1967) has long argued, simple redistribution of land without reform measures that extend to educational facilities, credit institutions, or market mechanisms is ". . . likely to prove disappointing to nearly everyone concerned." As the now-extensive literature on land reform in Latin America indicates, reform within a tradition-bound constitutional framework is painfully slow. Whether violent revolution is perceived as a precondition for effective land reform depends on one's view of the power structure. G. C. Botero (1970) argues that no government dominated by large landowners is likely to introduce a reform which will effectively deprive that class of the economic and social basis of its power, and any attempt to change the agrarian structure without touching the power structure will fail. To exemplify his point, Botero points out that between 1961 and June 1969, title deeds for 88,200 properties (2,800,000 hectares) were delivered in Colombia but that 91 percent of these titles, representing 95.9 percent of the total land, related not to expropriation of land but to legal recognition of existing ownership. Of 105,000 hectares expropriated, only 13,400 hectares have been distributed to 1,194 persons.

Happily, it does not appear that Botero's viewpoint can be generalized to Latin America as a whole. First, almost all governments have agrarian reform laws on the books, and redistribution of land over the last five to six years has been rapid. Second, the majority of Latin American countries endorse the United Nations General Assembly resolutions on agrarian reform (FAO 1971, p. 4):

> Agrarian reform is . . . a simple and logical outcome of the general statements on the aims of international organizations contained in the San Francisco Charter and since supplemented by basic documents such as the Universal Declaration of Human Rights, covenants connected with those rights, and Resolution 2542 of the Twenty-Fourth Session of the United Nations General Assembly on Social Progress and Development. . . . the above mentioned declaration on Social Progress and Development, which was approved unanimously by the General Assembly, clearly states that such progress and development requires the participation of all members of society in a productive and socially useful task and the establishment of patterns of land ownership and of means of production that exclude any forms of exploitation of human beings and create conditions of true equality among them.

Possibly the most up-to-date information on agrarian reform progress has been collected by FAO and the German Foundation for International Development and was presented at the Consultation of Experts on the Development of Agrarian Structure in Latin America, Berlin, November, 1973. For example, the Institute of Agricultural Development in Chile (INDAP) reported that by September 1973, 9,861,516 hectares of irrigated and dry land had been expropriated and redistributed to 59,659 families. The National Center for Training and Research in Agrarian Reform in Peru

(CENCIRA) reported that by October 1973 over 40 million hectares of the best-quality land in the country had been expropriated and assigned to some 190,000 families.

One of the most significant findings of the meeting of experts was that government officials, researchers, and peasants alike felt that allocation of small parcels of land to single households (to be operated individually and in isolation) was not particularly conducive to modernization of agriculture and to desired improvements in standards of living of the peasantry. As an alternative, most countries favored associative tenure and/or production arrangements. Emerging arrangements which proved to have both staying power and at least satisfactory performance included "group farming settlements (asentamientos), peasant committees and socialized production centers" in Chile, "communal enterprises" in Colombia, "agrarian production co-operatives, communal co-operatives and restructured traditional peasant communities" in Peru, "communal enterprises" in Costa Rica, "agricultural workers' production co-operatives" in Argentina, "agricultural co-operatives with individual home gardens" in the Dominican Republic, "individual plots in integrated agricultural settlement development projects" in Brazil, "collective ejidos and co-operatives" in Mexico, "agrarian centers, co-operatives and borrowers' unions" in Venezuela, and "agricultural producers co-operatives, communes, colonies and rural land societies" in Ecuador.

A central feature in the design of all of these cooperative arrangements is (1) communal control of the land (though not always tenure control), (2) preferential value assigned to labor over other factors of production, and (3) elevation of campesinos in the entrepreneurial control of the production process through self- or co-management.

Possibly the most comprehensive coverage on the problems of policy that governments must face in implementing land reform is to be found in the ongoing Praeger studies of agricultural development in the economies of Latin America (E.A. Duff 1968, L.E. Heaton 1969, D. Heath, C. Eramus, and H. Buechler 1969, D.F. Fienup, R.H. Brannon, and F.A. Fender 1969, A.K. Ludwig and H.W. Taylor 1969, A.J. Contu and R.A. King 1969, G.E. Schuh 1970). As for the innumerable problems in designing an effective land reform program, the reader is referred to the excellent work of the Land Tenure Center of the University of Wisconsin.

6. Summary and Conclusions

THE OBJECTIVE of this study has been to propose a theoretical model of determinants of out-migration from the rural sectors of a number of Latin American economies. The model applies to countries with high rates of population increase and in which the structure of land tenure is characterized by a large proportion of the rural-agricultural population belonging to the minifundio and landless employee class and large proportions of the agricultural land held by latifundios. Basic to the derivation of the model is the claim that the distribution of agricultural labor to land resources is institutionally inflexible and that rigidities within the "minifundio-latifundio complex" have conditioned the cost of land, its use, availability, and development to the extent that social and economic opportunities for the majority of the rural population have been stifled. In other terms, labor is subject to diminishing marginal returns because of the institutional system of land tenure which, in combination with rapid population growth, has caused conditions of economic stress to evolve, followed by high rates of rural emigration.

The empirical relevance of the model has been evaluated on the basis of the experience of Chile, 1952-60; Peru, 1940-61; Costa Rica, 1950-63; and Colombia, 1951-64. At the provincial level multiple-regression techniques and graphic analysis have been applied both separately for each country, and comparatively. Using a dependent/independent-variable format, the role of rural-agricultural conditions in migration has been evaluated absolutely (e.g., stocks and flows of population pressure on the land, agricultural wages and unemployment, literacy, and amenities) and relatively (e.g., urban-rural wage, employment, and amenity differentials).

While some of the hypotheses tested are exploratory in nature, most test some aspect of the theoretical model. The most important hypothesis relates to derived stock and flow indexes of population pressure and agricultural inopportunity. These indexes take into consideration effects of latifundio landholding on both availability of land to the rural "poor" and employment prospects for minifundio and landless workers. In both Chile and Peru, only those variables concerned with production possibilities and population pressure within the minifundio-latifundio complex were significantly and consistently related to measures of provincial out-migration. In the case of Chile the regressions accounted for $R^2 = 0.74$ of the variation in the dependent variable; in the case of Peru, $R^2 = 0.67$. The experience of Colombia and Costa Rica also added support to the theoretical model and hypotheses. With a much more even distribution of labor to land in Costa Rica, rates of out-migration were observed to be much lower. A final look at the rural migration experience of sixteen Latin American countries compared to their structure of land tenure adds further support to the model.

At the very least, this study is a methodological exercise resulting in one more demonstration of the need for land redistribution. It also supplements largely descriptive demographic analyses of differentials and selectivity in migration. It is relevant for policy in its focus on the system of land tenure as part and parcel of a host of conditions within the minifundio-latifundio complex which tend to restrict utilization of potentially productive resources and spur out-migration as a result.

Admittedly, the line of causation extending from the theoretical model to the empirical correlations is uneven. Inferences, based on the empirical correlations, that land redistribution per se will result in more employment opportunities and less migration run the risk of being in error. As discussed in the theoretical model, reform of the minifundio-latifundio complex embodies more than just redistribution of land. This has become painfully evident in the reforms of Chile, Peru, and Colombia, where employment and income redistribution expectations have been only partially met because beneficiaries of land redistribution refuse to allow more families onto the land, and small individual farm units have encountered great difficulties in obtaining credit and finding satisfactory markets. In other terms, the implied link between rural emigration and land redistribution must be anchored to objectives of full employment, small-farm credit programs, more adequate market mechanisms for minifundio products, and extension programs for members of the minifundio and landless employee class. With this qualification in mind, the major claim of this study is that agrarian reform and land redistribution will have beneficial side effects such as slowing rural-urban migration and reducing open unemployment in cities and strain on the urban infrastructure.

In the interests of further research along the lines of this study, it is important to acknowledge that the domain of the theoretical model is rather narrow. Focus is primarily on the income-earning opportunities of male household heads with the presumption that forces acting to bring about their migration will operate in like manner for their dependents, and to some extent for females. The theoretical model also lacks rigor in that it is more of a descriptive model than one enabling logico-deductive predictions. By the same token, the correspondence between the theoretical model and the empirical model lacks rigor due largely to inadequate statistical data for the measurement of concepts.

Of course, the inquiry is by no means conclusive. Both theoretically and empirically, it might be described as exploratory in the sense that few studies have addressed the kinds of issues raised here. An obvious concern for future research will be to ascertain whether the empirical findings for Chile, Peru, Costa Rica, and Colombia are corroborated in other contexts, i.e., at provincial levels in other Latin American countries or for smaller units of analysis in any of the four sample countries. The study is also inconclusive when it comes to evaluating the ramifications of land reform and land redistribution on levels of rural-agricultural living and consequently on rural out-migration behavior. Unfortunately, census data may not facilitate this kind of evaluation for some time, since the effects of recent agrarian reforms (i.e., over the last six years) may be only partially represented in the statistics of the 1970 censuses of agriculture. It would seem that adequate testing of these interactions may require extensive field study of migration in areas currently experiencing dissolution of the minifundio-latifundio complex.

Finally, it may be that the author's concern with influencing rural-urban migration in the process of Latin American growth and development has been too ambitious. It would certainly have been overambitious to expect to answer all of the questions raised on the basis of empirical evidence from available aggregate statistical sources. This study may claim, however, to have addressed policy and planning issues of critical importance in present-day Latin America. As revealed by the United Nations World Population Conference, the United Nations Second Population Inquiry, and numerous academic writings, policy makers are hard-pressed for answers to questions about (1) ways of stimulating, halting, or diverting rural-urban migration flows and (2) possible inefficiencies in the performance of the labor market as a "mechanism" for the effective distribution of the economy's labor resources. In attempting to explain the causes of rural out-migration in Latin America, we have addressed one important facet of this issue and in examining possibilities for manipulating those causes we have indicated that the implications of this inquiry are of pragmatic worth.

Appendix I

Notes on the "Components of Intercensal Population
and Labor-Force Change Technique"

This technique is useful for estimating the rural-urban migration of population cohorts over censal periods. To illustrate, the data requirements and assumptions for a Chilean population cohort aged 20-24 in 1950 and 30-34 in 1960 are provided below. Exemplary data computations are given in Table 1.

Data Requirements

1. Census of Chile population and labor-force data for 1952 by age and sex groups (preferably five-year intervals). Linear interpolation of the above to the year 1950.
2. Census of Chile data on the above for 1960.
3. Population and labor-force counts and labor-force activity rates for the 1950 and 1960 total, urban, and rural population data.

Assumptions

1. The census mortality rate for the country is adequate for both the urban and rural populations.
2. Labor-force mortality will equal population mortality.
3. The age-sex specific activity rates for the migrant population are the same as those for the nonmigrants.
4. International emigration or immigration is not significant over the period.
5. Enumeration is equally complete or equally incomplete at the time of both censuses.

Table 1. Example of the "Components of Intercensal Population and Labor-Force Change Technique" for a Cohort Aged 20-24 in 1950 and 30-34 in 1960

	Chile Total	Rural Total	Total Males	Rural Males	Total Females	Rural Females
Population						
1. 1950 (000s)	517.8	194.3	252.9	104.3	264.9	90.0
2. 1960 (000s)	507.2	136.6	246.9	74.4	260.3	62.4
3. Change (000s)	-10.6	-57.7	-6.0	-29.9	-4.6	-27.6
4. Average (000s)	512.5	165.5	249.9	89.4	262.6	76.2
Labor-Force						
5. 1950 (000s)	322.9	110.6	232.1	96.4	94.9	16.1
6. 1960 (000s)	302.6	78.4	244.1	73.2	61.8	5.2
7. Change (000s)	-21.3	-32.2	12.0	-23.2	-33.1	-10.9
8. Average (000s)	313.3	94.5	238.1	84.8	78.4	10.7
Activity Rates						
9. 1950	0.6255	0.5692	0.9177	0.9242	0.3582	0.1788
10. 1960	0.5966	0.5734	0.9886	0.9838	0.2374	0.0833
11. Change	-0.0289	0.0047	0.0709	0.0596	-0.1208	-0.0955
12. Average	0.6110	0.5716	0.9532	0.9540	0.2978	0.1310
Components of Population Change						
13. Intercensal death rate (3/4)	-0.0207		-0.0240		-0.0175	
14. Deaths (13 x 14)	-10.6	-3.4	-6.0	-2.2	-4.6	-1.3
15. Net migration (3 - 14)	0	-54.3	0	-27.7	0	-26.3
Components of Labor-Force Change						
16. Deaths (14 x 12)	-6.5	-1.9	-5.7	-2.1	-1.4	-0.2
17. Net migration (15 x 12)	0	-31.0	0	-26.4	0	-3.4

18. Accessions and retirements (11 x 4)	-14.8	17.8	17.7	-5.3	-31.7	-7.2
19. Sum of 16, 17, and 18	-21.3	-32.2	12.0	-23.2	-33.1	-10.7
20. Discrepancy due to rounding (7 - 19)	0	0	0	0	0	0

Appendix II

Derivation of Rates of Net Provincial Rural Male
Labor-Force Migration

In this Appendix, steps for estimating rates of net provincial rural male labor-force migration are outlined. The data for Chile, Peru, Costa Rica, and Colombia are shown in Tables 1-4, respectively. Data sources for the calculations are provided in Table 5.

Using statistics of the provincial rural population at the time of the first census (column 1, Table 1, for Chile), an average provincial rate of natural increase for the census interval (column 4) is applied to column 1 and compounded for n years to arrive at an expected provincial rural population—in the absence of migration—at the end of the census interval. The average provincial rates of natural increase have been calculated using yearly provincial birth and death statistics for each country, since birth and death statistics were not available for the urban and rural parts of the province. Although this means a likely underestimate of the expected provincial rural population at the end of the census interval—given that rural rates of natural increase are normally higher than for urban areas—we may assume that these underestimates are evenly distributed by province. Whether the provincial birth and death rates are reliable depends on both the registration procedures and the extent to which registration laws are observed in each country during the respective census intervals. Questions of reliability are discussed in greater detail later.

138

Table 1. Derivation of Rates of Male Labor-Force Rural Out-Migration--Chile (1952-60)

Province	1[a]	2[b]	3[c]	4[d]	5[e]	6[f]	7[g]	8[h]	9[i]	10[j]	11[k]
Aconcagua	77,349	62,542	69,944	2.87	96,998	-33,032	47	0.46	0.5825	-13.1	-1.63
Valparaíso	73,455	69,029	71,242	2.55	89,848	-20,819	29	0.45	0.6036	- 7.9	-0.99
Santiago	233,123	243,459	238,291	2.92	293,483	-50,024	21	0.46	0.5663	- 5.5	-0.68
O'Higgins	133,766	121,155	127,460	2.97	169,056	-47,901	37	0.47	0.5825	-10.4	-1.30
Colchagua	103,030	106,686	104,858	2.91	129,606	-22,920	22	0.48	0.5728	- 6.0	-0.75
Curicó	56,100	62,443	59,271	2.86	70,297	-7,854	13	0.47	0.5851	- 3.6	-0.45
Talca	105,175	116,332	110,753	2.60	129,149	-12,817	12	0.46	0.5878	- 3.2	-0.40
Maule	45,695	47,968	46,831	2.38	55,156	-7,188	15	0.48	0.5623	- 4.0	-0.50
Linares	101,987	109,093	105,540	2.56	124,844	-15,751	15	0.47	0.5769	- 4.1	-0.51
Ñuble	163,401	172,480	167,940	2.40	197,540	-25,060	15	0.48	0.5673	- 4.1	-0.51
Bío-Bío	94,146	106,088	100,117	2.55	115,156	-99,068	9	0.47	0.5570	- 2.4	-0.30
Malleco	97,772	95,950	96,861	2.41	118,291	-22,341	23	0.47	0.5580	- 6.0	-0.75
Cautín	244,149	241,758	242,953	1.60	276,249	-34,491	14	0.48	0.5314	- 3.4	-0.42
Osorno	73,288	77,588	75,437	2.28	87,770	-10,182	13	0.47	0.5770	- 3.5	-0.43
Llanquihue	94,793	97,324	96,058	2.53	115,767	-18,443	19	0.49	0.5420	- 5.0	-0.62

a. Total rural population, 1952.

b. Total rural population, 1960.

c. Total rural average population, 1952-60 (1 + 2/2).

d. Average rate of rural natural increase, 1952-60, r.

e. Expected total rural population, 1960, due to compound r x 1.

f. Net population rural migration, 1952-60 (2 - 5).

g. Rate of total rural population out-migration per 100, 1952-60 (6/3).

h. Estimated proportion of total rural migrants that are males, 1952-60.

i. Average rural male activity rates, 1952-60.

j. Rate of rural male labor-force out-migration (7 x 8 x 9).

k. Average yearly rate of rural male labor-force out-migration (10/8 years).

Table 2. Derivation of Rates of Male Labor-Force Rural Out-Migration--Peru (1940-61)

Province	1[a]	2[b]	3[c]	2.9[l]	3.8[m]	3.8[n]	5[e]	6[f]	7[g]	8[h]	9[i]	10[j]	11[k]
					4[d]								
Tumbes	15,467	22,600	19,038	2.9	3.8	3.8	31,866	- 9,266	-48.0	0.483	0.4965	-11.5	-0.55
Piura	278,409	384,100	331,254	3.0	3.1	3.5	534,780	-151,680	-45.7	0.497	0.4926	-11.2	-0.53
Cajamarca	463,342	668,000	565,671	1.4	1.8	2.9	706,821	38,821	- 6.7	0.513	0.4804	- 1.7	-0.08
Lambayeque	97,807	135,100	116,453	3.0	3.6	3.1	190,791	- 55,691	-47.8	0.481	0.4932	-11.3	-0.53
La Libertad	278,811	354,900	316,855	2.0	2.5	2.8	494,264	-139,364	-44.0	0.500	0.4982	-11.0	-0.52
Ancash	359,148	404,500	381,824	1.5	1.9	2.8	551,703	-147,203	-38.6	0.522	0.4807	- 9.7	-0.46
Huánuco	204,917	273,000	238,958	0.5	1.0	1.9	261,333	+ 11,669	+ 4.9	0.501	0.4879	+ 1.2	+0.06
Junín	240,642	273,900	257,271	1.7	2.1	2.6	374,826	-100,926	-39.2	0.502	0.5114	-10.1	-0.48
Lima	203,361	287,400	245,380	1.8	2.7	2.9	339,159	- 51,759	-21.1	0.467	0.5459	- 5.4	-0.25
Ica	80,811	120,700	100,750	1.2	2.8	2.9	130,760	- 10,060	-10.0	0.462	0.5472	- 2.5	-0.12
Huancavelica	224,722	255,000	240,111	1.0	1.1	2.0	298,782	- 43,282	-17.3	0.515	0.4736	- 4.2	-0.20
Ayacucho	300,553	320,000	310,276	0.4	0.7	1.8	367,704	- 47,704	-15.4	0.532	0.4624	- 3.8	-0.18
Cuzco	404,748	436,200	420,474	1.0	1.2	2.0	541,875	-105,675	-25.1	0.500	0.5330	- 6.7	-0.32
Apurímac	240,378	243,400	241,889	1.2	1.3	2.3	335,393	- 91,993	-38.0	0.528	0.4601	- 9.2	-0.44
Puno	554,462	595,100	574,781	1.1	1.4	1.8	747,532	-152,432	-26.5	0.525	0.4860	- 6.8	-0.32
Moquegua	27,016	27,900	27,458	1.6	2.0	2.5	40,857	-113,399	-48.6	0.496	0.5094	-12.1	-0.58
Tacna	17,633	20,600	19,117	1.1	1.8	3.0	26,526	- 5,974	-31.3	0.440	0.5991	- 8.3	-0.39
Loreto	122,723	218,500	170,611	2.2	2.5	2.4	200,562	+ 17,938	+10.5	0.473	0.4624	+ 2.3	+0.11
San Martín	44,785	69,500	57,142	2.2	2.5	3.0	75,720	- 6,220	-10.9	0.492	0.4426	- 2.4	-0.11

a. Total rural population, 1940.

b. Total rural population, 1961.

c. Total rural average population, 1940-61 (1 + 2/2).

d. Average rate of rural natural increase, 1940-61, r.

e. Expected total rural population, 1961, due to compound $r \times 1$.

f. Net population rural migration, 1940-61 (2 - 5).

g. Rate of total rural population out-migration per 100, 1940-61 (6/3).

h. Estimated proportion of total rural migrants that are males, 1940-61.

i. Average rural male activity rates, 1940-61.

j. Rate of rural male labor-force out-migration (7 x 8 x 9).

k. Average yearly rate of rural male labor-force out-migration (10/21 years).

l. Average rate of rural natural increase, 1940-47.

m. Average rate of rural natural increase, 1948-54.

n. Average rate of rural natural increase, 1955-61.

Table 3. Derivation of Rates of Male Labor-Force Rural Out-Migration--Costa Rica (1950-63)

Province	1[a]	2[b]	3[c]	4[d]		5[e]	6[f]	7[g]	8[h]	9[i]	10[j]	11[k]
Alajuela	119,882	196,607	156,245	3.6[l]	4.4[m]	199,923	- 3,316	- 2.1	0.49	0.513	-0.53	-0.04
Cartago	76,248	116,027	96,137	3.8	4.4	128,115	-12,088	-12.6	0.48	0.513	-3.10	-0.23
Heredia	34,531	55,860	45,145	3.5	4.3	56,777	- 917	- 2.0	0.50	0.507	-0.51	-0.03
Guanacaste	76,218	121,196	98,707	4.5	4.8	137,676	-16,480	-16.7	0.48	0.489	-3.50	-0.30
Puntarenas	63,795	122,470	93,132	4.8	4.9	118,090	4,380	+ 4.7	0.48	0.524	+1.28	+0.09
Limón	29,724	45,813	37,768	3.8	4.1	50,711	- 4,888	-13.0	0.47	0.550	-3.54	-0.27

a. Total rural population, 1950.

b. Total rural population, 1963.

c. Total rural average population, 1950-63 $(1 + 2/2)$.

d. Average rate of rural natural increase, 1950-63, compounded r.

e. Expected total rural population, 1963, due to compound $r \times 1$.

f. Net population rural migration, 1950-63 $(2 - 5)$.

g. Rate of total rural population out-migration per 100, 1950-63 $(6/3)$.

h. Estimated proportion of total rural migrants that are males, 1950-63.

i. Average rural male activity rates, 1950-63.

j. Rate of rural male labor-force out-migration $(7 \times 8 \times 9)$.

k. Average yearly rate of rural male labor-force out-migration (10/13 years).

l. Average rate of rural natural increase, 1950-57.

m. Average rate of rural natural increase, 1958-63.

Table 4. Derivation of Rates of Male Labor Force Rural Out-Migration—Colombia (1951-64)

Province	1[a]	2[b]	3[c]	4[d]	5[e]	6[f]	7[g]
Antioquia	933,158	1,106,118	1,019,638	3.77	1,509,693	-403,575	-40
Atlántico	39,365	45,952	42,659	3.36	60,491	- 15,068	-35
Bolívar	504,078	402,313	453,196	2.83	724,529	-322,216	-71
Boyacá	694,314	863,626	778,970	2.91	1,008,102	-144,476	-19
Cauca	323,932	474,070	399,001	2.41	441,473	32,597	8
Cundinamarca	791,412	831,058	811,235	3.40	1,222,276	-391,218	-48
Huila	208,602	245,325	226,964	2.99	305,952	- 60,627	-27
Magdalena	236,672	365,427	301,050	2.87	341,901	- 23,525	8
Nariño	436,453	514,873	475,663	2.51	602,419	- 87,436	-18
Notre de Santander	248,508	274,680	261,594	3.52	389,633	-114,953	-44
Santander	526,424	579,072	552,748	2.90	763,371	-184,299	-33
Tolima	475,383	478,303	476,843	2.22	632,426	-154,123	-32

a. Total rural population, 1951.

b. Total rural population, 1964.

c. Total rural average population, 1951-64 $(1 + 2/2)$.

d. Average rate of rural natural increase, 1951-64, compounded r.

e. Expected total rural population, 1964, due to compound $r \times 1$.

f. Net population rural migration, 1951-64 $(2 - 5)$.

g. Rate of total rural population out-migration per 100, 1951-64 $(6/3)$.

Table 5. Data Sources

Chile

Population and labor-force data

Censo General de Población (1952, 1960), Dirección de Estadística y Censos, Chile.

Provincial population rates of natural increase

Boletín de Estadísticas Demográficas (1952-60), no. 6, Dirección de Estadística y Censos, and computed from 1960 Census of Population.

Peru

Population and labor-force data

Censo Nacional de Población y Ocupación (1940), Ministerio de Hacienda y Comercio, Lima, 1944.

Sexto Censo Nacional de Población (1961), Instituto Nacional de Planificación, Lima, 1964.

Centros Poblados (1961), Dirección Nacional de Estadística y Censos, vol. 1-4, Lima, 1966.

Provincial rates of natural increase

Anuario Estadístico del Perú (1940-53, 1966), Ministerio de Hacienda y Comercio.

Costa Rica

Population and labor-force data

Censo de Población de Costa Rica (1950) and *Censo de Vivienda* (1963), Ministerio de Economía y Hacienda, Dirección de Estadística y Censos, San José.

Rates of provincial natural increase

Anuario Estadístico (1950-63), Ministerio de Economía y Hacienda, Dirección de Estadística y Censos.

Colombia

Population data

Censo de Población (1951, 1964), Departamento Administrativo Nacional de Estadística Resumé, Colombia.

Given the expected provincial rural population estimate—in the absence of migration—at the end of the census interval, the net provincial population migrating over the census interval (column 6) can be estimated by subtracting the expected population (column 5) from the actual provincial rural population at the end of the census interval (column 2). This estimate is transformed to a rate per 100 (column 7) by dividing the average provincial rural population at risk (column 3) by the estimated net provincial rural migrants (column 6).

In estimating provincial net population migration, it is important to acknowledge two limitations. First, we may assume that the estimate of rural net out-migration includes international as well as internal movements—the balance of in-and-out movements—but that international migration into the rural part of each province is probably infinitesimal. Second, the estimates include the effects of rural-urban reclassification, which may exaggerate net migration to an extent which doubtless varies among provinces and is probably greatest where urbanization is progressing most rapidly.

On the basis of international migration statistics for each country, the preceding assumption is highly reasonable. The second consideration poses problems, however. In both Chile and Peru, a population center is classified as urban, not on the basis of sheer numbers, but rather on the criterion that it demonstrates an urban character. Accordingly, it has not been possible to isolate reclassified areas over the census interval for Chile and Peru or to adjust for the effect of the reclassifications in the estimates of rural migration. As the census interval for Peru spans some twenty years, we may expect this problem to be most significant in the accuracy of the magnitudes of both the provincial and national rates of rural out-migration.

The next step is to estimate the proportion of the net provincial rural population migrants that are both males and economically active. To do this, we (1) calculate the average proportion of males present in the rural population over the census interval, (2) assume that originally there was a one-to-one sex ratio of live births, (3) subtract the rates in (1) from unity to arrive at an estimate of the proportion of net migrants that must be males (column 8), (4) calculate the average provincial rural male activity rates over the census interval (column 9), and (5) multiply the estimate of the provincial rural net population migrants that must be males (column 8) times the proportion of those males in the provincial labor force (column

9) and column 7 to get a rate of net provincial rural male labor-force migration (column 10). Finally, the total net rates in column 10 for the census interval are divided by the number of years in the census interval to arrive at average yearly rates of net provincial rural male labor-force migration (column 11).

From a methodological viewpoint, procedures 2, 3, and 5, above, may be open to error. In procedure 2, we assume a live birth-sex ratio of one male to one female. In Chile, 1952-60, the ratio is actually 1.05, whereas in Peru, the ratio is approximately 1.01. The differences are, however, slight, and, unless variations are considered at the provincial level (which they are not), a constant sex ratio of 1 to 1 or 1.05 to 1 for all provinces will not affect the regression results.

In procedure 3, differences in mortality rates between males and females are not taken into consideration. That is, although an actual ratio of live male births to live female births may be 1.05 to 1 in Chile, this ratio will not persist in the same order for all age groups as mortality differentials for males and females affect the sex balance. On the basis of 1960 life table data for Peru, Chile, Venezuela, and Colombia (N. Keyfitz and W. Flieger 1968), approximately 1.05 to 1.07 males die to every 1.00 females over the age span 0-50 years. Again, this discrepancy is slight and may actually serve as a corrective mechanism in cases where the sex ratio estimate is in error.

Procedure 5 ignores variations of migration rates according to age and labor-force participation. That is, after estimating the proportion of rural out-migrants that must be males, we may estimate the proportion that must be in the labor force by assuming that migrants in the labor force are represented in the same proportions in the migration stream as they are in the original rural population.

To evaluate whether this assumption (and, therefore, procedure 5) is reasonable, rural population and labor-force out-migrants were calculated for the ages 5-54 in 1950 and 15-64 in 1960 for Chile using a "components of intercensal population and labor-force change technique" (that is, incorporating a census survival ratio method and age-specific activity rates) and the estimation procedures described above. For the "components of intercensal population and labor-force change technique," 242,200 rural population out-migrants and 183,600 rural labor-force out-migrants were calculated. For the estimation procedures used in this Appendix, 251,980 rural population out-migrants and 176,400 rural labor-force out-migrants were calculated. Using the "components of intercensal population and labor-force change technique" procedure as a standard, this method produced a 3.9 percent overestimate for rural population out-migrants and a 4.1 percent underestimate for rural labor-force out-migrants. Clearly the deviations are very small, indicating that the method used is not too imprecise. Evaluating the degree to which the two methods correspond at the provincial level, however, is another matter. First, only for Chile are the required data available for this "components technique" for both the beginning and end of the census interval. Second, the "components technique" is complex and requires a great many calculations. The evaluation of the procedures used in this Appendix (that is, for Chile at the national level) do not indicate that the choice of a more complex, time-consuming method would result in substantially improved migration estimates.

To a considerable extent, the accuracy of the estimates of net provincial rural male labor-force migration depends on the reliability of the provincial birth and death rates—that is, the reliability of the registration procedures and the extent to which registration laws are observed in each country. An indirect way of evaluating the reliability of provincial birth and death rates is to compare a country's annual rate of natural increase between time t and $t+n$ with the national census population growth rate calculated from the national censuses of time t and $t+n$. This step has been undertaken in Table 1.2 (pp. 6-7) for Chile and Peru. That is, the annual population growth rate indicated by the censuses (including net international migration) is 2.5 percent for both Chile, 1952-60, and Peru, 1940-61. On the other hand, as indicated by the registered births and deaths, the national rate of natural increase per 1,000 population per year was 24.5 for Chile, 1952-60, and 22.3 for Peru, 1940-61.

For Chile, then, calculations at the national level using the rate of natural increase appear to correspond closely with the intercensal growth rate. For Peru, however, there is an appreciable discrepancy, which suggests the possibility of the birth and death data underestimating the true rate of natural increase. The rate of 25/1,000 suggested by the census may well be a better estimate. On that basis, the estimate of net rural out-migration for Peru as a whole would be increased by about 175,000 (as against 1,480,765 as indicated in Table 1.2).

In the case of Costa Rica, correspondence between the annual rate of natural increase indicated by the birth and death data and the annual population growth rate indicated by the census is much like that of Chile. In both cases the growth rate is approximately 4.0 percent (or 40/1,000). Actually, use of Costa Rica's annual rate of natural increase (as against the census growth rate) slightly underestimates the number of rural population out-migrants by approximately 1,750 (that is, 38,044 as against 39,700), or by 4.6 percent.

Admittedly the above means of evaluation provide only a general idea of the reliability of the provincial birth and death rates used in the provincial net migration estimates. Unfortunately the same procedure cannot be used at the provincial level as provincial census population counts cannot be assumed closed to in- or out-migration (and, to date, cannot be adjusted accordingly by direct provincial migration counts). Therefore, provincial growth rates in the absence of migration cannot be calculated from the census, but can only be calculated indirectly using birth and death data.

To some extent, however, it is possible to evaluate the reliability of provincial birth and death data (and, therefore, the registration procedures) on the grounds of credibility. Of course, this approach presumes that registration birth and death data have not been modified before publication to reflect intercensal growth rates.

In Table 6, changes in rates of natural increase due to changes in live births and deaths for Peru, 1944-53, and Costa Rica, 1950-63, are given. Particularly in the case of Peru, some of these changes do not seem to be credible. For example, in the Peruvian provinces of Ica, Lima, and Loreto and the Costa Rican provinces of Heredia and San José, there are significant variations in yearly live birth rates (for example, from 30/1,000 for the first year to 43/1,000 for the second year to 33/1,000 for the third year). In such cases it is very likely that the reported quantities are a function of year-to-year variations in the quality of the registration machinery (particularly as it pertains to reported births). In calculating average annual provincial rates of natural increase for each of the sample countries, these problems were handled in two ways. First, where a range of yearly birth or death rates indicates a trend and this trend is broken at some point by a single major variation, the deviant case is excluded from the calculated average annual provincial rate of natural increase. For example, in the series of live births per 1,000 population for the Costa Rican provinces of Alajuela and Heredia, the enclosed rates have been eliminated from the calculated average annual birth rate:

Table 6. Changes in Rates of Natural Increase Due to Changes in Live Birth Rates and Death Rates for Peru (1944-53) and Costa Rica (1950-63)

Province	Changes in Crude Birth Rate 1944-53	Changes in Crude Death Rate 1944-53	Changes in Rate of Natural Increase 1944-53
Peru[a]			
Tumbes	+7.7	-1.6	+ 9.3
Piura	-0.1	-2.1	+ 2.0
Cajamarca	+3.7	-1.2	+ 4.9
Lambayeque	+3.6	-2.1	+ 5.7
La Libertad	+5.3	-0.8	+ 6.1
Ancash	+2.5	-2.8	+ 5.3
Huánuco	+5.6	-0.7	+ 6.3
Junín	+4.7	-3.8	+ 8.5
Lima	+9.5	-3.5	+13.0
Ica	+20.1	-2.4	+22.4
Huancavelica	-0.4	-2.2	+ 1.8
Ayacucho	+1.0	-1.8	+ 2.8
Cuzco	-0.4	-0.8	+ 0.4
Apurímac	-2.4	-1.0	- 1.4
Arequipa	+6.2	-0.9	+ 7.2
Puno	-0.5	-0.6	+ 0.1
Moquegua	+1.0	-2.0	+ 3.0
Tacna	+2.8	-3.1	+ 5.9
Loreto	+8.0	-3.1	+11.1
San Martín	+6.3	-4.0	+10.3
Madre de Dios	+0.1	-3.0	+ 3.1

Costa Rica[b]	1950–63	1951–63	1950–63
Alajuela	+ 5.0	-3.4	+ 8.4
Cartago	+ 4.3	-2.4	+ 6.7
Heredia	+11.1	-2.5	+13.6
Guanacaste	- 0.3	-2.6	+ 2.3
Puntarenas	- 4.1	-6.2	+ 2.1
Limón	+ 2.7	-2.4	+ 5.1
San José	+ 6.2	-1.5	+ 7.7

a. *Anuario Estadístico Perú*, Ministerio de Hacienda y Comercio (1948–55 and 1966).

b. *Anuario Estadístico*, Dirección General de Estadística y Censos (1964).

	1960	1959	1958	1957	1956	1955	1954	1953
Alajuela	51.9	50.2	48.0	(61.4)	51.3	49.4	49.6	45.4
Heredia	(58.0)	46.9	46.7	52.1	48.3	49.1	49.3	43.6

In contrast, the death rate series is generally much more even:

	1960	1959	1958	1957	1956	1955	1954	1953
Alajuela	7.8	8.9	8.6	9.5	9.2	9.9	10.0	11.9
Heredia	8.3	8.2	7.9	8.7	9.0	10.1	9.3	10.3

Second, where the trend is uneven (and sometimes questionable), it has been necessary to assume that an average annual rate of natural increase balances out errors and that between provinces, this balancing out of errors results in a set of average provincial annual growth rates in which errors are evenly distributed.

At the same time, even though errors are assumed to be normally distributed, this does not eliminate the strong possibility that provincial rates of natural increase—based on the birth and death rates—include errors. For example, referring again to the preceding exemplary birth rates for Costa Rica, the fact that significant yearly variations occur suggests that all of the rates may be in error to some extent (for example, ± 1 or 2 points). If this is the case, both the accuracy of the calculated net migration rates and, consequently, the resulting correlations in the multiple-regression and graphic analyses would be influenced.

Appendix III

Values for the Derivation of the Stock and Flow
Indexes of Population Pressure and
Agricultural Inopportunity

In this Appendix, data values and procedures used in the derivation of the stock and flow indexes are given. One calculation which requires clarification in the derivation of both indexes concerns the stock and flow estimate of the component $f(L_0 + L_w + F_0)$, which represents the rural population dependent upon latifundios and intermediate-sized farms for means of livelihood. The problem concerns the time reference for which census data are available. In Chile and Costa Rica, agricultural data are available for the year 1955; in Colombia, for 1960; and in Peru, for 1961 (Tables 1-4). Thus, for Chile, Costa Rica, and Colombia, the actual census data are for a year between t and $t + n$, whereas for Peru data are for year $t + n$. In the stock estimate, however, estimates of $f(L_0 + L_w + F_0)$ are required for the beginning of the time interval—at time t corresponding to P_t. Therefore, it has been necessary to interpolate backwards to time t using a yearly compound growth operator.

The only growth operator available is the rural provincial rate of natural increase r, which is applied as $(1/r)^n$ to $f(L_0 + L_w + F_0)$ for the n years required to "arrive" at $f(L_0 + L_w + F_0)_t$—a stock estimate. In turn, to derive a flow estimate from $f(L_0 + L_w + F_0)_t$ to $t + n$, we simply apply the same population growth operator, $(1 + r)^n$.

153

Table 1. Values for Chilean Provinces

Province	1[a]	2[b]	3[c]	4[d]	5[e]	6[f]
Aconcagua	6.0	2,753	62	887	88,590	65,200
Valparaíso	4.5	3,713	145	1,305	97,847	75,800
Santiago	4.8	8,305	329	3,865	323,422	215,600
O'Higgins	6.8	4,070	133	1,824	124,012	69,300
Colchagua	7.2	3,705	212	2,360	240,782	169,100
Curicó	6.6	1,243	110	1,555	107,031	48,900
Talca	6.5	4,058	206	2,593	243,810	90,300
Maule	6.4	617	191	3,768	140,833	56,300
Linares	6.7	3,250	216	3,330	253,600	158,400
Ñuble	6.4	3,083	439	9,090	533,756	237,400
Bío-Bío	6.8	4,384	292	5,187	331,938	200,200
Malleco	6.6	3,228	346	3,508	455,101	261,400
Cautín	6.3	4,030	451	12,138	807,742	374,900
Osorno	6.3	2,275	308	3,083	314,764	268,400
Llanquihue	6.8	805	278	7,083	233,313	153,800

a. Average provincial rural family size, 1952-60 (f).

b. Workers on latifundios, 1955 (L_w).

c. Latifundio owners, 1955 (L_O).

d. Intermediate-sized farms, 1955 (F_O).

e. Provincial arable agricultural land in hectares, 1955 (T_A).

f. Provincial arable agricultural land held by latifundistas in hectares, 1955 (L_A).

Table 2. Values for Costa Rican Provinces

Province	1^a	2^b	3^c	4^d	5^e	6^f
Alajuela	6.0	1,504	37	5,816	103,434	9,378
Cartago	6.2	2,643	32	1,664	40,464	7,896
Heredia	6.0	92	15	840	22,204	226
Guanacaste	6.4	1,474	73	6,763	119,190	15,401
Puntarenas	5.4	1,253	46	4,457	100,236	20,355
Limón	4.3	3,201	32	1,809	93,667	43,353

a. Average provincial rural family size, 1950–63 (f).

b. Workers on latifundios, 1955 (L_w).

c. Latifundio owners, 1955 (L_O).

d. Intermediate-sized farms, 1955 (F_O).

e. Provincial arable agricultural land in hectares, 1955 (T_A).

f. Provincial arable agricultural land held by latifundistas in hectares, 1955 (L_A).

Table 3. Values for Colombian Provinces

Province	1[a]	2[b]	3[c]	4[d]	5[e]	6[f]
Antioquia	5.62	1,958	747	49,177	547,169	58,603
Atlántico	3.40	200	71	3,917	34,963	1,000
Bolívar	4.88	1,272	614	23,328	201,919	37,543
Boyacá	3.94	1,185	743	44,000	426,305	15,675
Cauca	4.73	327	194	21,030	243,148	16,714
Cundinamarca	4.53	785	278	44,102	478,628	26,820
Huila	5.21	309	277	18,098	157,726	12,380
Magdalena	5.21	2,768	1,195	23,845	404,326	112,104
Nariño	4.92	38	56	29,496	298,546	7,914
Notre de Santander	5.35	259	103	23,882	250,251	10,854
Santander	4.93	662	466	43,380	485,173	47,692
Tolima	5.40	1,059	438	22,506	442,156	47,769

a. Average provincial rural family size, 1951–64 (f).

b. Workers on latifundios, 1960 (L_w).

c. Latifundio owners, 1960 (L_o).

d. Intermediate-sized farms, 1960 (F_o).

e. Provincial arable agricultural land in hectares, 1964 (T_A).

f. Provincial arable agricultural land held by latifundistas in hectares, 1964 (L_A).

Table 4. Values for Peruvian Provinces[a]

Province	1[b]	2[c]	3[d]	4[e]	5[f]
Tumbes	5.53	2	241	5,838	2,565
Piura	5.76	91	3,872	160,853	110,000
Cajamarca	5.22	189	22,135	290,629	121,800
Lambayeque	5.64	33	3,194	165,729	146,300
La Libertad	5.51	127	7,392	198,534	140,000
Ancash	4.74	219	7,832	209,556	106,240
Huánuco	5.03	132	10,759	120,909	49,000
Junín	4.75	148	6,120	127,449	62,000
Lima	4.86	205	6,530	177,226	105,300
Ica	5.68	52	1,939	92,174	43,000
Huancavelica	4.58	157	6,572	125,301	52,800
Ayacucho	5.10	151	8,242	130,124	39,600
Cuzco	5.08	469	7,839	168,047	90,000
Apurímac	4.65	106	3,477	77,956	38,700
Puno	4.49	908	17,793	151,164	73,600
Moquegua	4.36	13	447	22,815	15,317
Tacna	4.93	35	1,139	16,724	8,250
Loreto	6.50	49	3,945	142,236	23,560
San Martín	5.71	10	8,629	62,353	5,500

a. As pointed out in Chapter 4, footnote 6, p. 87, census data were not available for the component L_W (workers on latifundios) and, therefore, the numerator of the stock and flow indexes for Peru is $f(L_O + f_O)$ rather than $f(L_O + L_W + F_O)$.

b. Average provincial rural family size, 1940–61 (f).

c. Latifundio owners, 1961 (L_O).

d. Intermediate-sized farms, 1961 (F_O).

e. Provincial arable agricultural land in hectares, 1961 (T_A).

f. Provincial arable agricultural land held by latifundistas in hectares, 1961 (L_A).

The following example illustrates the procedures involved for the province of Aconcagua, Chile:[1]

$$\text{Stock Index} = \frac{P_t - f(L_w + L_o + F_o)}{T_A - L_A}$$

1. Stock of actual provincial population at $P_t = 1952$ 77,349
2. Population dependent on latifundios and intermediate-sized farms $f(L_w + L_o + F_o)_{1955}$ 22,050
3. $n = 1955 - 1952$ 3
4. $r =$ rate of provincial natural increase averaged from 1952 to 1960   2.87
5. Stock of $f(L_w + L_o + F_o)_{1952} = $ line $2(1 - r)^n$ or line $2(1 - \text{line } 4)^n$ 20,151
6. Stock of population demands on the land $= P_{1952} - f(L_w + L_o + F_o)_{1952}$ or line 1 $-$ line 5   57,198
7. Provincial arable agricultural land (T_A) 88,590
8. Provincial arable agricultural land held by latifundistas (L_A) 65,200
9. $T_A - L_A$ or line 7 $-$ line 8   23,390
10. Stock index line 6/line 9   2.45

$$\text{Flow Index} = \frac{P_t(1 + r)^n - P_t - f(L_w + L_o + F_o)_t(1 + r)^n - f(L_w + L_o + F_o)}{T_A - L_A}$$

1. Stock of actual provincial population at $P_t = 1952$ 77,349
2. Expected population in rural sector at $P_{t+n} =$ 1960 in absence of migration $=$ $P_t(1 + r)^n$, where $r = 2.87$ and $n = 8$ 96,998
3. Growth in rural population in absence of migration (that is, flow) from 1952 to 1960 or line 1 $-$ line 2   19,649
4. Stock of $f(L_w + L_o + F_o)_t$ in 1952 (as calculated to the left)   20,151
5. Expected $f(L_w + L_o + F_o)_{t+n}$, where $t + n = 1960$ $=$ line $4(1 + r)^n$, where $r = 2.87$ and $n = 8$ 25,270
6. Growth of $f(L_w + L_o + F_o)$ from 1952 to 1960 in absence of migration (that is, flow)   5,119
7. Numerator representing the flow of rural population or line 3 $-$ line 6   14,530

1. See Appendix II for values of P_t, r, and $P_t(1 + r)^n$.

8. Provincial arable agricultural land (T_A) 88,590
9. Provincial arable agricultural land held by
   latifundistas (L_A) 65,200
10. $T_A - L_A$ or line 8 − line 9 = denominator   23,390
11. Flow index line 7/line 10   0.62

Appendix IV

Notes on Weighted Multiple-Regression Analysis

Aside from the usual precautions in using regression analysis (see J. Johnston 1963, R. P. Shaw 1974a), considerable care must be exercised in choosing units of analysis. This is sometimes referred to as an "ecological problem" and is present in the regressions on Chilean and Peruvian migration. To illustrate, consider the units of analysis for the Peruvian regressions. First, data are available only at the rural provincial level. As nineteen provinces have been included in the regressions, there are nineteen units or "observations." Accordingly, since the main concern is to account for variation in the incidence of rural out-migration in terms of the incidence of various structural characteristics of each province, the dependent and independent variables are expressed as rates (usually per 100 population or labor force).

Now, although rates per 100 rural provincial population or labor force are comparable for the nineteen units of analysis, the significance of any particular rate in the country's total rural-urban migration flow, or its absolute importance relative to any other province's rate, is dependent on the relative population size of each unit of analysis. Unless steps are taken to weight the units of analysis to compensate for this type of difference, the regression line may be misleading in relation to policy. To illustrate, consider the six hypothetical observations and the hypothetical regression line in Figure 1.

160

Figure 1

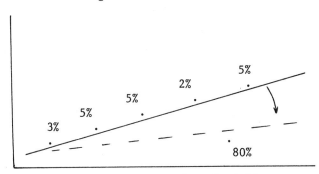

Value of Independent Variable

Each point represents a rate of out-migration and a value for the independent variable. The percentage values represent the proportion of the country's population in each unit of analysis (provinces are each represented by a dot in the figure). On the basis of the points alone (i.e., unweighted analysis), the regression line would imply a high correlation between the dependent and independent variable and would "predict" that a change in the independent variable would affect the dependent variable considerably.

If policy considerations are being formulated, manipulation of the independent variable (e.g., increasing literacy) would be expected to have considerable significance in altering the "behavior" of the dependent variable. Yet for the country's population represented by the points on the regression line, this does not prove to be the case. One way of handling this problem (and the measure adopted in the regressions) is to weight each observation proportionately to its share of the total sample size. For example, if the smallest unit of analysis accounts for 2 percent of the sample population yet occupies one point on the regression line, then the largest unit of analysis, which accounts for 80 percent of the sample population, should occupy $(80/2) = 40$ points on the regression line. If this adjustment were made in Figure 1, the regression line would swing downward, indicating little relationship between the independent and dependent variable. In effect, this procedure standardizes the size of each unit of analysis. Although this procedure is obviously inferior to having more evenly sized units of analysis in the first place (preferably to the household level), it is clear that consideration should be given to the need for weighting when it is not possible to control for the size of the units in the regression analysis.

Appendix V

Values for the Independent Variables Used in Regressions
for Chile and Peru, and Data Sources for Independent
Variables for Chile, Peru, Costa Rica, and Colombia

Tables 1 and 2 present values for the independent variables used in regressions for Chile and Peru.

In most cases, calculation of values in this Appendix is straightforward and is based on census data. For the agricultural and rural-urban wage data for Peru and Costa Rica, values are calculated averages from median wage and salary data as reported in census sources. For the urban-rural amenity variables, differentials have been calculated as multiples—that is, an urban value divided by a rural value.

Data sources for the independent variables for Chile, Peru, Costa Rica, and Colombia are given in Table 3.

Table 1. Values for the Independent Variables--Chile

Province	C_1	C_2	C_3	C_4	C_{5a}	C_{5b}	C_6	C_7	C_8	C_9	C_{10}	C_{11}	C_{12}	C_{13}
Aconcagua	64.6	74.3	0.57	80.9	2.45	0.62	99.4	11.0	2.02	29.8	5.4	1.24	47.4	19.6
Valparaíso	70.1	88.0	0.60	81.0	2.37	0.53	107.7	17.0	4.77	26.4	5.4	1.29	86.9	22.6
Santiago	56.3	73.6	0.43	84.1	1.66	0.43	109.6	-5.0	2.54	28.5	5.8	1.30	88.5	24.1
O'Higgins	71.8	79.6	0.66	89.3	1.85	0.52	93.6	2.8	2.04	33.4	5.0	1.30	46.7	15.3
Colchagua	67.1	73.2	0.48	87.3	0.87	0.23	79.4	30.0	2.00	40.3	6.6	1.40	29.3	13.2
Curicó	41.3	76.8	0.32	85.1	0.67	0.15	80.7	10.0	1.80	40.9	8.3	1.43	39.0	12.7
Talca	26.5	52.1	0.18	84.6	0.42	0.13	84.8	5.4	2.14	39.3	8.3	1.45	41.3	11.6
Maule	19.4	76.6	0.11	60.6	0.23	0.05	70.0	-0.2	2.51	38.1	7.3	1.37	38.4	6.5
Linares	42.9	61.7	0.25	81.6	0.60	0.14	66.8	14.0	2.20	36.0	9.9	1.31	33.1	13.4
Ñuble	37.0	72.9	0.24	66.3	0.30	0.08	70.7	36.5	3.55	38.5	9.8	1.36	37.3	6.9
Bío-Bío	25.9	70.7	0.12	70.9	0.25	0.05	71.6	17.4	2.44	37.1	9.7	1.32	37.5	10.1
Malleco	16.3	39.3	0.05	57.9	0.29	0.06	92.9	-13.0	2.06	41.6	9.1	1.43	42.0	8.6
Cautín	17.9	68.0	0.04	35.7	0.34	0.04	90.0	- 1.0	4.62	36.3	10.0	1.37	35.8	8.6
Osorno	23.4	58.7	0.11	68.8	0.85	0.18	93.2	- 1.6	1.96	27.3	7.6	1.18	43.0	18.5
Llanquihue	17.4	56.5	0.09	46.6	0.57	0.13	99.3	- 1.8	1.29	25.9	7.1	1.16	37.0	10.3

Key:
C_1 = % of provincial farm holdings having less than 5 hectares (minifundios), 1955.
C_2 = % of provincial agricultural land held by farms greater than 500 hectares (latifundios), 1955.
C_3 = % of provincial agricultural labor force on farms having less than 5 hectares weighted by average provincial population growth rates, 1952-60.
C_4 = Average % of provincial labor force employees and productive workers, 1952-60.
C_{5a} = Stock index of rural population pressure and agricultural inopportunity.
C_{5b} = Flow index of rural population pressure and agricultural inopportunity.
C_6 = Average provincial agricultural wage, 1952-60.
C_7 = % of change in provincial agricultural wage, 1952-60.
C_8 = Average provincial urban wage index as a multiple of average provincial rural wage index, 1960.
C_9 = Average % of provincial rural male population illiterate, 1952-60.
C_{10} = Provincial urban housing shortage, 1960, as a multiple of same for rural, 1960.
C_{11} = Average % of provincial urban population literate as a multiple of same for rural, 1952-60.
C_{12} = Average % of provincial population classified as urban, 1952-60.
C_{13} = Number of cars, buses, and trucks per 1,000 provincial population, 1960.

Table 2. Values for the Independent Variables--Peru

Province	P_1	P_2	P_3	P_4	P_{5a}	P_{5b}	P_6	P_7	P_8	P_9	P_{10}	P_{11}
Tumbes	92.4	88.0	0.70	47.0	4.62	4.62	102.7	1.09	19.8	1.44	1.2	51.5
Piura	90.0	82.2	0.52	49.0	5.32	4.76	88.2	1.67	47.5	1.76	2.3	40.5
Cajamarca	79.9	59.2	0.42	17.8	2.34	1.15	63.6	2.09	33.0	1.71	1.9	14.4
Lambayeque	76.0	82.6	0.36	74.1	4.72	4.16	88.9	1.67	35.7	2.52	1.6	55.9
La Libertad	78.4	84.4	0.32	40.0	4.47	3.26	123.2	1.17	24.3	1.17	1.7	35.9
Ancash	89.3	74.3	0.48	27.7	3.27	1.70	74.5	2.37	45.4	1.03	2.1	28.1
Huánuco	77.5	63.0	0.21	27.3	2.26	0.61	50.9	1.21	41.8	1.26	2.4	19.9
Junín	88.8	76.6	0.48	31.3	3.42	1.86	103.9	1.48	28.6	1.20	1.5	45.0
Lima	84.2	75.3	0.35	57.7	2.65	1.32	134.5	1.83	14.0	1.07	1.1	81.4
Ica	73.0	49.0	0.17	83.2	1.52	0.90	119.5	1.26	14.5	1.23	1.2	48.0
Huancavelica	91.1	68.8	0.36	14.0	2.80	0.89	18.8	0.90	69.4	1.23	2.0	17.3
Ayacucho	88.0	56.3	0.27	14.3	2.97	0.62	38.4	2.33	61.2	1.40	2.3	24.6
Cuzco	88.0	81.1	0.27	26.5	4.76	1.58	29.3	1.39	13.3	1.21	2.9	28.8
Apurímac	93.0	82.3	0.36	16.3	5.84	2.28	28.9	2.14	68.1	1.17	2.8	17.1
Puno	83.6	80.0	0.29	25.4	6.38	2.17	29.0	2.18	60.6	1.20	2.5	15.6
Moquegua	93.0	90.0	0.40	24.5	3.45	1.66	84.0	2.19	30.3	1.00	1.7	36.1
Tacna	75.1	70.0	0.52	41.1	1.68	0.76	75.4	1.76	27.8	1.45	1.3	61.4
Loreto	82.2	66.7	0.38	22.0	0.92	0.64	90.2	1.30	20.4	2.00	1.5	35.5
San Martín	31.2	9.2	0.24	12.5	0.40	0.07	67.5	1.69	32.5	2.83	1.4	57.4

Key: P_1 = % of provincial farm holdings having less than 5 hectares (minifundios), 1961.
 P_2 = % of provincial agricultural land held by farms having more than 500 hectares (latifundios), 1961.
 P_3 = % of provincial agricultural labor force on minifundios weighted by average provincial population rates of natural increase, 1940-61.
 P_4 = % of provincial agricultural labor force employees and productive workers, 1961.
 P_{5a} = Stock index of rural provincial population pressure and agricultural inopportunity.

P_{5b} = Flow index of rural provincial population pressure and agricultural inopportunity.

P_6 = Provincial median weekly agricultural workers salary, 1961.

P_7 = Provincial median urban salary as a multiple of provincial median rural salary, 1961.

P_8 = % of provincial rural male population aged 15 years and over illiterate, 1961.

P_9 = Index of provincial urban housing quality as multiple of same for rural, 1961.

P_{10} = Average % of provincial urban population literate as multiple of same for rural, 1940–61.

P_{11} = Average % of provincial population classified as urban, 1940–61.

Table 3. Data Sources for Independent Variables for Chile, Peru, Costa Rica, and Colombia

Chile

Agricultural data--variables C_1, C_2, C_3, C_4, C_5 *III Censo Nacional Agrícola Ganadero*, Vol. I-V, Ministerio de Economía y Dirección de Estadística y Censos

Population and labor force data--variables C_5, C_{12} *1952* and *1960*, XII and XIII *Censo de Población*, Dirección de Estadística y Censos

Birth and death statistics--variable C_5 *1952-60 Demografía*, Dirección de Estadística y Censos

Average agricultural wage data--variables C_6, C_7 F. S. Weaver, *Regional Patterns of Economic Change in Chile 1950-64*, Cornell University, Latin American Program Study No. 11, 1968

Urban-rural wage data--variable C_8 *XIII Censo de Población y Antecedentes Básicos para la Regionalización y Decentralización de Chile*, Oficina de Planificación Nacional, Santiago, Chile, 1966

Urban-rural illiteracy data--variables C_9, C_{10} *Algunos Antecedentes para el Planeamiento*, Ministerio de Educación Pública, 1960

Urban-rural housing data--variable C_{10} *Antecedentes Básicos para la Regionalización y Decentralización de Chile*, Oficina de Planificación Nacional, and XIII Censos de Población, 1960

Transportation data--variable C_{13} *Comercio Exterior y Comunicaciones*, Dirección de Estadística y Censos, 1960, Chile

Peru

Agricultural data--variables P_1, P_2, P_3, P_4, P_5 *Primer Censo Nacional Agropecuario*, 1961, Instituto Nacional de Planificación, Dirección Nacional de Estadística y Censos, 1961, Lima

Population and labor-force data--variables P_5,P_8,P_{10},P_{11}

1940 *Censo Nacional de Población y Ocupación*, Ministerio de Hacienda y Comercio, Lima, 1944; *Centros Poblados, 1961*, Dirección Nacional de Estadística y Censos; *Sexto Censo Nacional de Estadística y Censos*, Tomo II, 1964, Lima; *1966 Anuario Estadístico del Perú*, Ministerio de Hacienda y Comercio

Birth and death statistics--variable P_5

1948-55, 1966, *Anuario Estadístico del Perú*, Ministerio de Hacienda y Comercio

Agricultural wage--variable P_6

1961 *Boletín de Estadística Peruana*, *Estadística Económica y Financiera*, Dirección Nacional de Estadística y Censos, Lima, 1964

Urban-rural wage data--variable P_7

1961 *Censo de Población*, Tomo IV

Urban-rural housing data--variable P_8

1964 *Primer Censo Nacional de Vivienda Instituto Nacional de Planificación*, Dirección Nacional de Estadística y Censos

Costa Rica

Agricultural data

1955 *Censo Agropecuario*, Ministerio de Economía y Hacienda, Dirección General de Estadística y Censos, San José, 1955; 1963 *Censo Agropecuario*, Dirección General de Estadística y Censos, Ministerio de Economía y Hacienda, 1965

Birth and death data

Anuario Estadístico, Dirección General de Estadística y Censos, 1964

Wage data

1958 *Estadística de Salarios*, Dirección General de Estadística y Censos

Housing data

Censos de 1963 de Población y Vivienda, Ministerio de Industria y Comercio, Dirección General de Estadística y Censos

Population and labor-force data

Censo de Población de 1950, Ministerio de Economía y Hacienda Dirección General de Estadística y Censos, San José, 1955; *1963 Censo de Población*, Dirección General de Estadística y Censos, Ministerio de Economía y Hacienda, 1960

Colombia

Agricultural data

Encuesta Agropecuaria Nacional de 1954, Departamento Administrativo Nacional de Estadística; *Nacional de Explotaciones Agropecuarias (Censo Agropecuario), 1960*, Departamento Administrativo Nacional de Estadística, 1962

Population data

Censo de Población de 1951, de 1964, Departamento Administrativo Nacional de Estadística

Bibliography

Adams, D. W.: Colombia's land tenure system: antecedents and problems, *Land Economics*, 42, 1966.

_____: Resource allocation in traditional agriculture: comment, *Journal of Farm Economics*, 49, 1967.

_____: Rural migration and agricultural development in Colombia, *Economic Development and Cultural Change*, 17, 1969.

_____: The economics of land reform, *Food Research Institute Studies*, 12, 1973.

Adams, D. W., and Montero, L. E.: Land parcelization in agrarian reform: a Colombian example, *Inter-American Economic Affairs*, 19, 1965.

Adams, D. W., and Schulman, S.: Minifundia in agrarian reform: a Colombian example, *Land Economics*, 43, 1967.

Antecedentes Básicos para La Regionalización y Decentralización de Chile. CORFO, Departamento de Planificación, Chile, 1964.

Arriaga, E.: *New Life Tables for Latin American Populations in the Nineteenth and Twentieth Centuries.* University of California at Berkeley Monograph Series, No. 3, 1968.

Barraclough, S.: Agrarian policy and land reform, *Journal of Political Economy*, 78, 1970.

Barraclough, S., and Domike, A. L.: Agrarian structure in seven Latin American countries, *Land Economics*, 42, 1966.

Barriaga, C.: Chile: peasants, politics and land reform, *LTC Newsletter*, 36, 1972.

Beals, R. E., and Menzes, C. I.: Migrant labour and agricultural output in Ghana, *Oxford Economic Papers*, 22, 1970.

Berry, R. A.: Land distribution, income distribution and the productive efficiency of Colombian agriculture, *Food Research Institute Studies*, 12, 1973.

Block, E. W., and Iutaka, S.: Rural-urban migration and social mobility: the controversy on Latin America, *Rural Sociology*, 34, 1969.

Bodenjofer, H. J.: The mobility of labor and the theory of human capital, *Journal of Human Resources*, 2, 1967.

Boserup, E.: *The Conditions of Agricultural Growth.* Aldine, 1967.

Botero, G. C.: La réforme agraire en Colombie, *Civilisations*, 20, 1970.

Brannon, R. H.: Low investment levels in Uruguayan agriculture: some tentative explanations, *Land Economics*, 45, 1969.

Bray, J. O.: Demand and the supply of food in Chile, *Journal of Farm Economics*, 44, 1962.

_____: Mechanization and the Chilean inquilino system; the case of fundio B, *Land Economics*, 42, 1966.

Brennan, M. J.: A more general theory of resource migration, in M. J. Brennan (ed.), *Patterns of Resource Behavior*. Brown, 1965.

Browning, H. L., and Feindt, W.: Selectivity of migrants to a metropolis in a developing country: a Mexican case study, *Demography*, 6, 1969.

Burke, M.: An analysis of the Bolivian land reform by means of a comparison between Peruvian haciendas and Bolivian ex-haciendas, Unpublished Ph.D. thesis, Microfilmed Ann Arbor, 1968.

Caldwell, J. C.: *African Rural-Urban Migration*. Columbia University Press, 1970.

Camacho-Saa, C.: Minifundia, productivity and land reform in Cochabamba, Bolivia, Unpublished Ph.D. thesis, Microfilmed Ann Arbor, 1967.

Camisa, Z. C.: Effects of migration on the growth and structure of population in the cities of Latin America, *United Nations World Population Conference*, 4, 1965.

Carrol, T. F., Felix, D., and Grunwald, J.: (respective chapters in) A. O. Hirschman (ed.), *Latin American Issues, Essays and Comments*. Twentieth Century Fund, 1961.

CEPAL-FAO, *Análisis de Algunos Factores que Obstaculizan el Incremento de la Producción Agropecuaria*. E/CN, 12/306, FAO, 1953.

Chaplin, D.: *The Peruvian Industrial Labor Force*. Princeton University Press, 1967.

Chenery, H. B.: Patterns of industrial growth, *American Economic Review*, 50, 1960.

Cheung, S.: *The Theory of Share Tenancy*. University of Chicago Press, 1969.

Chile: Demand and Supply Projections for Agricultural Products: 1965-1980. Catholic University of Chile, Economic Research Center, 1969.

Chirikos, T. N., *et al.*: *Human Resources in Bolivia*. Center for Human Resources Research, Ohio State University, 1971.

CIDA: *Tenencia de la Tierra y Desarrollo Socio-Económico del Sector Agrícola*. Volumes on Argentina (A. Domike), Brazil (E. Feder and M. Sund), Colombia (E. Shearer, O. Delgado and F. Herrero), Chile (M. Sternberg, J. D. Canto, C. Talavera, and J. C. Collarte), Ecuador (R. Baranona), Guatemala (S. M. Cats and E. Venezian), Peru (A. Saco, R. Leits and S. P. Reyes). Inter-American Committee for Agricultural Development, Pan American Union, 1966.

Clark, R. J.: Land reform and peasant market participation in the north highlands of Bolivia, *Land Economics*, 44, 1968.

Clement, N. C.: The economic viability of the Mexican ejido: a case study of three ejidos in Jalisco, Unpublished Ph.D. thesis, Microfilmed Ann Arbor, 1968.

Cline, W. R.: *Economic Consequences of a Land Reform in Brazil*. North-Holland Publishing Company, 1970.

Coffey, J. D.: Impact of technology on traditional agriculture: the Peru case, *Journal of Farm Economics*, 49, 1967.

Coutu, A. J., and King, R. A.: *The Agricultural Development of Peru*. Praeger, 1969.

Crosson, P. R.: *Agricultural Development and Productivity: Lessons from the Chilean Experience*. Johns Hopkins Press, 1970.

Davis, K.: The theory of change and response in modern demographic history, *Population Index*, 24, 1963.

Delgado, O. (ed.): *Reformas Agrarias en la América Latina*. Fondo de Cultura Económica, Mexico, 1961.

Desarrollo Económico de Chile: 1940-56. Instituto de Economía de la Universidad de Chile, 1956.

Diehl, W. D.: Farm-nonfarm migration in the southeast: a costs-returns analysis, *Journal of Farm Economics*, 48, 1966.

Dorner, P., and Felstehausen, L.: Agrarian reform and employment: the Colombian case, *International Labour Review*, 102, 1970.

Dorner, P., Brown, M., and Kanel, D.: Land tenure and reform: issues in Latin American development, *LTC Newsletter*, 29, 1969.

Dorner, P., *et al.*: *Agrarian Reform in the Dominican Republic.* University of Wisconsin Land Tenure Center Report, 1967.

Dovring, F.: Economic results of labor reform, *War Hunger*, 4, 1970a.

_____: Land reform and productivity in Mexico, *Land Economics*, 46, 1970b.

Ducoff, L. J.: The role of migration in the demographic development of Latin America, *Milbank Memorial Fund Quarterly*, 43, 1965.

Duff, E. A.: *Agrarian Reform in Colombia.* Praeger, 1968.

Durand, J. D., and Holden, K. C.: *Methods for Analyzing Components of Change in Size and Structure of the Labor Force.* University of Pennsylvania Population Studies Center Analytical and Technical Report No. 8, 1969.

Durand, J. D., and Miller, A. R.: *Methods of Analyzing Census Data on Economic Activities of the Population.* United Nations, ST/SOA/Ser. A/43, 1969.

Durand, J. D., and Pelaez, C. A.: Patterns of urbanization in Latin America, *Milbank Memorial Fund Quarterly*, 43, 1965.

Easterlin, R. A.: Towards a socio-economic theory of fertility: a survey of recent research on economic factors in American fertility, in S. J. Behrman *et al.*, *Fertility and Family Planning: A World View.* University of Michigan, 1969.

_____: Effects of agrarian population pressure: some prospective lines of analysis, Prepared for UNECAFE, Comparative Study of Population Growth and Agricultural Change, Bangkok, 1971.

El Mercurio: Situación de la agricultura y reforma agraria, April 22, Santiago, Chile, 1966.

Eldridge, H. T., and Thomas, D. S.: *Population Redistribution and Economic Growth, U. S.: 1870-1950.* Vol. 3, American Philosophical Society, 1964.

Elizaga, J.: The demographic aspects of unemployment and underemployment in Latin America, *United Nations World Population Conference*, vol. 4, Belgrade, 1965.

_____: A study of migration to greater Santiago, *Demography*, 3, 1966.

_____: Some brief notes on migratory movements to urban centers in Latin America, Unpublished Manuscript (n.d.).

Esser, K.: Agrarreform, ein macht-problem—zum herrschafts system der landherren in Chile, *Vierteljahnesberichte* (Hanover), 39, 1970.

Estudio Sobre Tenencia de la Tierra en Chile. Comité Inter-Americano de Desarrollo Agrícola, Santiago, 1964.

FAO: *Report of the Special Committee on Agrarian Reform.* Rome, 1971.

FAO-IBRD: *The Agricultural Development of Peru.* Washington, D. C., 1959.

Feder, E.: Land reform under the alliance for progress, *Journal of Farm Economics*, 47, 1964.

_____: The campesino is still waiting, half the land is held by 1% of the rural families, *Ceres*, 2, 1969.

Fei, J., and Ranis, G.: Innovation, capital accumulation and economic development, *American Economic Review*, 53, 1963.

_____: *Development of the Labor Surplus Economy.* R. D. Irwin Inc., 1964.

_____: Agrarianism, dualism and economic development, in I. Adelman and E. Thorebeck (eds.), *The Theory and Design of Economic Development.* Johns Hopkins Press, 1966.

Fielding, A. J.: Internal migration and regional economic growth: a case study of France, *Urban Studies*, 3, 1966.

Fienup, D. F., Brannon, R. H., and Fender, F. A.: *The Agricultural Development of Argentina.* Praeger, 1969.

Fischlowitz, E.: Internal migration in Brazil, *International Migration Review*, 3, 1968.

Fitchett, D. A.: Agricultural land tenure arrangements on the northern coast of Peru, *Inter-American Journal of Economic Affairs*, 20, 1966.

Fletcher, L. B., and Merrill, W. C.: *Latin American Agricultural Development and Policies.* Iowa State University Press, 1968.

Fletcher, L. B., Graber, E., Merrill, W. C., and Thorbecke, E.: *Guatemala's Economic Development: The Role of Agriculture.* Iowa State University Press, 1970.

Fletschner, C., and Wierer, K.: The role of agricultural markets in agrarian reform and land settlement projects, *Land Reform, Land Settlement and Co-operatives,* 1, 1972.

Flinn, W., and Cartano, D.: A comparison of the migration process to an urban barrio and to a rural community: two case studies, *Inter-American Economic Affairs,* 24, 1970.

Flora, J. L.: *Elite Solidarity and Land Tenure in the Cauca Valley of Colombia.* Cornell University Latin American Studies Program Dissertation Series, 1971.

Flores, E.: La reforma agraria del Perú, *Trimestre Economique,* 37, 1970.

Ford Foundation, Report of the Ford Foundation urban and regional development advisory program in Chile, Unpublished, 1971.

Friedlander, S.: *Labor Migration and Economic Growth: A Case Study of Puerto Rico.* MIT Press, 1965.

Friedmann, J.: The strategy of deliberate urbanization, Centro Interdiciplinario de Desarrollo Urbano (CIDU), Universidad Católica de Chile, 1967.

————: The role of cities in national development, *American Behavioral Scientist,* 12, 1969.

Friedmann, J., and Lackington, T.: Hyperurbanization and national development in Chile: some hypotheses, *Urban Affairs Quarterly,* 1967.

Galloway, L. E.: The economics of labor mobility: an empirical analysis, *Western Economic Journal,* 5, 1967.

Gollas, M.: *Surplus Labor and Economic Development: The Guatemalan Case.* University of Wisconsin Land Tenure Center, Reprint 39, 1970.

Gordon, J. B.: Labor mobility and economic growth: the Central American experience—Costa Rica and El Salvador, *Economic Development and Cultural Change,* 17, 1969.

Graham, D. H.: Divergent and convergent regional economic growth and internal migration in Brazil, 1940-60, *Economic Development and Cultural Change,* 18, 1970.

Greenwood, M. J., and Gormerly, P. T.: A comparison of the determinants of white and non-white interstate migration, *Demography,* 8, 1971.

Haney, E.: The economic reorganization of minifundia in a highland community of Colombia, Unpublished Ph.D. Dissertation, University of Wisconsin, 1969.

Harris, J. R., and Todaro, M. P.: Migration, unemployment and development: a two sector analysis, *American Economic Review,* 60, 1970.

Hassan, M. F.: Unemployment in Latin America: causes and remedies, *American Journal of Economics and Sociology,* 32, 1973.

Hauser, P. M. (ed.): *Urbanization in Latin America.* ECLA, 1959.

Hautefernne, S.: Les structures et la réforme agraires Chiliennes, première partie, *Civilisations,* 20, 1970.

Heath, D., Eramus, C., and Buechler, H.: *Land Reform and Social Revolution in Bolivia.* Praeger, 1969.

Heaton, L. E.: *The Agricultural Development of Venezuela.* Praeger, 1969.

Herrick, B.: *Urban Migration and Economic Development in Chile.* MIT Press, 1965.

Hertford, R.: Sources of change in Mexican agricultural production; 1940-65, Unpublished Ph.D. Dissertation, Microfilmed Ann Arbor, 1969.

Heyduk, D.: Bolivia's land reform, *Inter-American Economic Affairs,* 27, 1973.

Higgens, B.: The city and economic development, in G. H. Beyer, *The Urban Explosion in Latin America: A Continent in Process of Modernization.* Cornell University Press, 1967.

Hirschman, A. O.: *The Strategy of Economic Development.* Yale University Press, 1958.

_____: Inflation in Chile, in A. O. Hirschman, *Journeys Toward Progress*. Twentieth Century Fund, 1961.

Holmberg, A. R., and Dobyns, H. F.: The Cornell program in Vicos, Peru, in C. R. Wharton, Jr. (ed.), *Subsistence Agriculture and Economic Development*. Aldine, 1969.

Horton, D. E.: Land reform and economic development in Latin America: the Mexican case, *Illinois Agricultural Economics*, 8, 1968.

_____: Efectos de la reforma agraria en cuatro haciendas Peruanas, *LTC Newsletter*, 38, 1972.

Jaspersen, F. Z.: *The Economic Impact of the Venezuelan Agrarian Reform*. Ann Arbor, 1969.

Johnston, J.: *Econometric Methods*. McGraw-Hill, 1963.

Jorgenson, D.: Development of a dual economy, *Economic Journal*, 81, 1961.

Karcel, H. G.: Select factors areally associated with population growth due to net migration, *Annals of the Association of American Geographers*, 53, 1963.

Kaufman, R. R.: *The Politics of Land Reform in Chile: 1950-70, Public Policy, Political Institutions and Social Change*. Cambridge University Press, 1972.

Keyfitz, N., and Flieger, W.: *World Population*. University of Chicago Press, 1968.

La Vivienda en el Peru. Organization of American States, 1963.

Lambert, J.: *Latin America: Social Structure and Policy Institutions*. University of California Press, 1968.

Lansing, J. B., and Mueller, E.: *The Geographical Mobility of Labor*. University of Michigan Press, 1967.

Lee, E. S., et al.: *Population Redistribution and Economic Growth, U.S., 1870-1950*. Vol. 1, American Philosophical Society, 1957.

Leonova, V. I.: Ararnia reforma v Peru osnova social ekonomiceskih preobrazovani, *Latinskaja Am Moskva*, 4, 1970.

Lewis, W. A.: Development with unlimited supplies of labour, *The Manchester School*, 22, 1954.

_____: *The Theory of Economic Growth*. Harper and Row, 1955.

Lowry, I. S.: *Migration and Metropolitan Growth: Two Analytical Models*. Chandler, 1966.

Ludwig, A. K., and Taylor, H.W.: *Brazil's New Agrarian Reform: An Evaluation of Its Property Classification and Tax Systems*. Praeger, 1969.

Mamalakis, M., and Reynolds, C. W. (eds.): *Essays on the Chilean Economy*. R. D. Irwin Inc., 1965.

McInnis, M.: Age, education and occupational differentials in inter-regional migration: some evidence for Canada, *Demography*, 9, 1971.

Mellor, J. W.: The subsistence farmer in traditional economies, in C. Wharton, Jr. (ed.), *Subsistence Agriculture and Economic Development*. Aldine, 1969.

Miracle, M., and Berry, L.: Migrant labor and economic development, *Oxford Economic Papers*, 22, 1970.

Moreina, P.: *Reforma Agraria, Una Experiencia en Guatemala*. Imprenta Universitaria Guatemala, 1963.

Mueller, M. W.: Changing patterns of agricultural output and productivity in the private and land reform sectors in Mexico, 1940-60, *Economic Development and Cultural Change*, 18, 1970.

Nakajima, C.: Subsistence and commercial family farms: some theoretical models of subjective equilibrium, in C. R. Wharton, Jr. (ed.), *Subsistence Agriculture and Economic Development*. Aldine, 1969.

Nelson, R. R., Schultz, T. P., and Slighton, R. L.: *Structural Change in a Developing Economy*. Princeton University Press, 1971.

Nisbet, C. T.: Money lending in rural areas of Latin America, *American Journal of Economics and Sociology*, 30, 1971.

____ (ed.): *Latin American Problems in Economic Development*. The Free Press, 1969.

Okun, B.: Interstate population migration and state income inequality: a simultaneous equation approach, *Economic Development and Cultural Change*, 16, 1968.

Oliver, F. R.: Interregional migration and unemployment, 1951-61, *Journal of the Royal Statistical Society*, Series A, 117, 1964.

Olsson, G.: Distance and human interaction: a migration study, *Geographical Analysis*, 47, 1965.

————: Migration and resettlement: some comments on action suggested by scientific models, Paper presented to South East Asian Development Advisory Groups, Mekong Committee, Washington, D.C., 1971.

Paulston, R. G.: Socio-cultural constraints on educational development in Peru, *Journal of Developing Areas*, 5, 1971.

Peinado, M.: Land reform in three communities of Cochabamba, Bolivia, Unpublished Ph.D. Dissertation, University of Wisconsin, 1969.

Portes, A.: The urban slum in Chile: types and correlates, *Land Economics*, 47, 1971.

Reye, U.: The Bolivian example: agrarian reform and economic development, *Intereconomics*, 6, 1967.

Riberio, J. P., and Wharton, C. R., Jr.: The ACAR program in Minas Gerais, Brazil, in C. R. Wharton, Jr. (ed.), *Subsistence Agriculture and Economic Development*. Aldine, 1969.

Rogers, T. W.: Differential net-migration patterns in the SMSA's of the southern U. S.: 1950-60, *International Migration*, 6, 1970.

Rutman, G. L.: Migration and economic opportunities in West Virginia: a statistical analysis, *Rural Sociology*, 35, 1970.

Saenz, C. J.: *Population Growth, Economic Progress and Opportunities on the Land: the Case of Costa Rica.* Ann Arbor, 1970.

Sahota, G. S.: An economic analysis of internal migration in Brazil, *Journal of Political Economy*, 76, 1968.

Sandilands, R. J.: *The Modernization of the Agricultural Sector and Rural-Urban Migration in Colombia.* University of Glasgow Institute of Latin American Studies Occasional Paper No. 1, 1968.

Sandoval, R.: Agrarian reform in Latin America, *Land Reform, Land Settlement and Cooperatives*, 2, 1972.

Sazanu, G. W., and Davis, H.: Land taxation and land reform, *Economic Development and Cultural Change*, 21, 1973.

Schuh, G. E.: *The Agricultural Development of Brazil.* Praeger, 1970.

Schultz, T. P.: Rural-urban migration in Colombia, *Review of Economics and Statistics*, 53, 1971.

Schultz, T. W.: *Transforming Traditional Agriculture.* Yale University Press, 1964.

————: *An Endeavor to Clarify the Economic Components Underlying Chilean Agriculture.* University of Chicago Office of Agricultural Economic Research, Paper No. 6603, 1966.

Schuman, H., Inkeles, A., and Smith, D. H.: Some psychological effects and non-effects of literacy in a new nation, *Economic Development and Cultural Change*, 16, 1967.

Shaw, R. P.: *Migration Theory and Fact.* Regional Science Research Institute, 1974a.

————: A note on cost-return calculations and decisions to migrate, *Population Studies*, 28, 1974b.

————: A conceptual model of rural-urban transition and reproductive behavior, *Rural Sociology*, 1974c.

Sjaastad, L. A.: Income and migration in the United States, Unpublished Ph.D. Dissertation, University of Chicago, 1961.

————: The costs and returns of human migration, *Journal of Political Economy*, 70, 1962.

Smith, T. L.: *Current Social Trends and Problems in Latin America*. University of Florida Press, 1957.

————: *Colombia: Social Structure and the Process of Development*. University of Florida Press, 1967.

———— (ed.): *Agrarian Reform in Latin America*. Knopf, 1965.

Snedecor, G.: *Statistical Methods*. Iowa University Press, 1967.

Speare, A., Jr.: A cost-benefit model of rural-to-urban migration in Taiwan, *Population Studies*, 25, 1970.

Sternberg, M. J.: Chilean land tenure and land reform, Unpublished Ph.D. Dissertation, University of California at Berkeley, 1962.

————: Gearing agrarian reform to employment objectives with particular reference to Latin America, *World Land Reform Conference*, Rome, WLF/66/8, 1966.

————: The economic impact of the latifundista, *Land Reform, Land Settlement and Co-operatives*, 1, 1970.

Taber, S.: Economic opportunity and urban orientation as a factor in Uganda migration, in *Geographical Papers*. University of East Africa, Social Science Council Conference, 1968.

Tarver, J. D.: Interstate migration differentials, *American Sociological Review*, 28, 1963.

Thiesenhusen, W. C.: *Agrarian Reform and Economic Development in Chile: Some Cases of Colonization*. University of Wisconsin Land Tenure Center Reprint 24, 1966.

————: Population growth and agricultural employment in Latin America, with some U. S. comparisons, *American Journal of Agricultural Economics*, 51, 1969.

————: Agrarian reform in Chile, *AID Spring Review of Land Reform*, 1970.

————: Latin America's employment problem, *Science*, 174, 1971.

————: Chile's experiments in agrarian reform: colonization projects revisited, *American Journal of Agricultural Economics*, 56, 1974.

Thiesenhusen, W. C., and Bray, J. O.: Profit margins in Chilean agriculture: a reply and a rejoinder, *Land Economics*, 43, 1967.

Thorbecke, E.: Unemployment and underemployment in Latin America, Paper prepared for the Inter-American Development Bank (mimeo), 1969.

Todaro, M. P.: A model of labor migration and urban unemployment in less developed countries, *American Economic Review*, 59, 1969.

United Nations, *Land Reform; Defects in Agrarian Structure as Obstacles to Economic Development*. E/2003/Rev.1 ST/ECA/11, 1951.

————: *Survey of Latin America*. ECLA, E/CN.12/767/Rev.1, 1966.

Vanderkamp, J.: Interregional mobility in Canada; a study of the time pattern of migration, *Canadian Journal of Economics*, 1, 1968.

Warriner, D.: *Land Reform in Principle and Practice*. London Publishing House, 1969.

————: Results of land reform in Asian and Latin American countries, *Food Research Institute Studies*, 12, 1973.

Weaver, F. S.: *Regional Patterns of Economic Change in Chile, 1950-64*. Cornell University Latin American Program Study No. 11, 1968.

Webb, P. B.: *Revolution and Land Reform—Mexico as a Model for Latin America*. Ann Arbor, 1970.

Weckstein, R. S.: Evaluating the Mexican land reform, *Economic Development and Cultural Change*, 18, 1970.

Wetering, H. Van de: The current state of land reform in Peru, *LTC Newsletter*, 1973.

Wharton, C. R., Jr.: *Subsistence Agriculture and Economic Development*. Aldine, 1969.

Whittenberger, R. L., and Havens, A. E.: *A Longitudinal Analysis of Three Small-Farm Communities in Colombia*. University of Wisconsin Land Tenure Center Report No. 87, 1973.

Wieber, K.: Analysis of agrarian structure and agrarian reform, *Land Reform, Land Settlement and Co-operatives*, 1, 1969.

Winkleman, D.: A case of the exodus of labor from agriculture: Minnesota, *Journal of Farm Economics*, 48, 1964.

Winkleman, D., and Hansen, D.: Idle land: an anomaly in Mexican resource use, *Land Economics*, 47, 1971.

Wolpert, J.: Behaviorial aspects in the decision to migrate, *Papers and Proceedings of the Regional Science Association*, 15, 1965.

——: Migration as an adjustment to environmental stress, *Journal of Social Issues*, 22, 1966.

——: Distance and directional bias in interurban migratory flows, *Annals of the Association of American Geographers*, 57, 1967.

Youmans, R., and Schuh, G. E.: An empirical study of the agricultural labor market in a developing country: Brazil, *American Journal of Agricultural Economics*, 50, 1968.

Ziche, J.: Agrarreform in Chile, 1965-70, *Z. Ausl. Landw.* (Frankfurt), 10, 1971.

Index